TH
BU

THE SECRETS TO TAKING CONTROL OF YOUR BODY, MONEY, CAREER & LIFE

JERMAINE
HARRIS

Onion Custard Publishing Ltd

The Rut Buster
The Secrets to Taking Control of Your Body, Money, Career and Life

Published in the United Kingdom by Onion Custard Publishing Ltd.
www.onioncustard.com
Twitter: @onioncustard
facebook.com/OnionCustardPublishing

Paperback Edition ISBN: 9781909129924

First Edition: May, 2014
Second Edition October 2014
Third Edition January 2016
Category: Non-Fiction / Personal Development

www.jermaine-harris.com
Email: jermaine@jermaine-harris.com

*Dedicated to the power of the decision that
will allow you to turn your life around.
Make that decision today.*

*Dedicated to my family, especially my beautiful mum, who showed incredible
patience during my formative years.*

*Dedicated to Rhydian Fairfax, a giant of
Personal Development who has kept me
accountable along my journey.*

*Dedicated to Anthony Robbins, your energy
and insights have allowed you to mentor me
from afar for many years.*

*Dedicated to James Robert Stevens,
the most incredible grandfather and mentor
any young man could ever hope for.
I will always serve in honour of your memory.*

*Most of all, dedicated to Katie Clarke,
who helped me to create a vision
of a fantastic future.
I love you beautiful.*

Part of the revenue from this book will support *Dementia UK,
Cancer Research UK* and *The British Heart Foundation.*

To

Kimberly

Your mission is inspiring
and it is going to
be amazing to watch it
unfold

X

CONTENTS

FOREWORD

The world is looking for young, inspiring leaders more than ever. It is the young people with real, actionable strategies who hold the future to our success. I believe we have found one of these individuals in Jermaine Harris. Jermaine's ability to take the greatest psychological, personal development, and self-help theories and turn them into simple, easy to follow strategies is remarkable.

I have had the absolute privilege of spending time with Jermaine, both in social and business settings. I am now proud to call him a dear friend. It is through my business associations with Jermaine that I have seen the tools outlined in this book used first hand. I have seen people escape from their rut just by spending ten minutes with him. I have watched Jermaine literally *transform* their thinking. This book narrows down Jermaine's best techniques so they can help you, today. In my time building successful businesses I have realised that even the most complex problems can have simple solutions. Jermaine's philosophy is the same.

Whatever area of your life is causing you to feel 'stuck' at this present time, you will discover that by using this book as a guide you can overcome it, and enjoy the road of continuous self-improvement.

This is your opportunity to allow Jermaine to help you to transform your life in the same way he did with mine. Grab the opportunity with both hands and enjoy the ride. Your life could be about to change forever.

Matt Travis

Mastery Trading Academy

INTRODUCTION

This book contains the tools and strategies you'll need to transform yourself and your destiny. While this may seem an outrageous thing to say, so many people across the world (including myself) have been completely amazed by what can happen when you use proven strategies to take control of your life.

It's time for you to finally take control of your life, starting now. I have the right to say that the information in this book, when acted upon, will change your life because I haven't personally invented anything to create the book. I have merely put together a system that uses a combination of some of the greatest personal development ideas in history.

You may of course think that some of the ideas in this book are 'crazy' or 'would never work'. All I'll say to that is this – you have been looking for ways to improve your life and, for whatever reason, what you have tried so far hasn't worked, so please be open minded and allow the techniques inside this book to change your life for the better.

I want you to imagine an old, slightly shaky rope bridge. You are on one side and the life that you really want is on the other, and the only way you can get to the other side is with my help. I want you to picture the fact that it seems a bit crazy to take even the first step, but for some reason let's say you really do trust me… and you do it. As you take each easy step it seems less crazy and you become excited by the fact that you are going to get to the other side. When you get there you really do feel grateful and congratulate yourself on having taken that crazy first step. **100% of people who don't take the first step will never get there.**

This book has been designed with the idea in mind that, on average, we only remember 10% of what we have read two weeks after we read it. However, that statistic can jump well above 80% when it comes to remembering things that we have written down, visualized and actually done. That being said, you will need a pen or a pencil and an active imagination as you go through this book because you are actually going to be doing things. (If you have an electronic version of this book use a notepad for the writing exercises). Think of this book as a metaphor for life. What I mean by that is this – you cannot build a multi-million dollar company or a stunning physique just by reading about it, you are going to have to **do** something.

The following information is simple by design, it is supposed to be a quick, actionable guide for you to get out of the hole you're in so you can start your continuous improvement. Certain bits of information will be repeated; this is deliberate, because there are some things that we need to hear a few times before they stick.

Only 1% of people ever finish the longer self-help books. *The Rut Buster* is deliberately written to be snappy, with bite-sized chapters. Quick to read, but with stimulating exercises that engage you. It's not a theory book. You need to break your childhood resistance to writing in books. It's allowed, in fact in this book it's essential!

It is crucial to realise that people do not just 'escape their rut' or 'transform their lives' by chance. They achieve predictable results by changing their thought patterns and the things they do, every day. I am going to share with you these patterns of thinking and acting, and how to use them to improve your life.

> "It always seems impossible until it is done."
>
> **Nelson Mandela**

Is it Really Possible for Me to Change My Life?

The minute you make the decision to change your life, it is already changed forever. Your life really can change in an instant. That moment you say 'I do', the moment your child was born, the job you nearly didn't apply for.

If you recall a time when your life changed in a matter of moments, you realise how your ultimate destination in life was completely altered as a result. Imagine the possibilities when you actually take control of these moments, and ultimately take control of your life's destination – your destiny.

The strategies contained in *The Rut Buster* are cutting edge. Why? They are a culmination of all of the greatest happiness, success and fulfilment techniques ever created. Every time you take action on the new information you will make small changes. Changes you may not even be aware of. As these changes start to stack up on top of each other you will become aware of how much you have changed, and how much your life has improved.

You may not believe every chapter is applicable to you right now. For example, you may be perfectly happy with your career and finances, but not so happy with your health and relationships. That's fine - I encourage you to use this book as a guide that you can turn to, in order to improve any area of your life at any given time. However, I believe that one key to happiness is progress and even if one area of your life is good, it can always improve, so why not read the whole book? You may pick up some ideas to make your life even better.

I'm sure you have heard of the benefits of persistence. With a little persistence, you will be like the rocket that uses 80% of its fuel just to get off the ground. In this universe, big changes need big amounts of energy, so be prepared to invest your heart and soul into improving your life. Just like the rocket you will climb to heights that you previously viewed as impossible.

When the Wright brothers first suggested the possibility of flight they were seen by their friends and family as totally insane. Make no mistake, these people were saying this out of love and they didn't want them to waste their time. Luckily for all of us the Wright brothers refused to give in just because other people couldn't see the revolutionary future of air travel that they did. Due to their persistence, a few decades later (and after some other humans caught on to the possibilities of air travel) we can now get from London to New York in seven hours while lying in bed and watching a movie. I cannot help but wonder how many human breakthroughs and opportunities to live extraordinary lives have been quashed by well-meaning loved ones.

Countless numbers of people have used the strategies presented in this book to catapult themselves to amazing success and happiness from exactly where you are right now, or from even worse situations! There is a catch, however. For the techniques in this book to work I am going to need you to commit to playing at 100%, 80% just won't cut it. You have nothing to lose and everything to gain. Be bold, be brave and be fantastic. Finally, be prepared to close your ears to the well-meaning advice of others, and stay committed to your journey of self-improvement, because some of the ideas may seem crazy at first - but hey, so did the aeroplane...

My Story

People will ridicule your journey, and then be in awe of your destination.

Whilst juggling University, an overactive social life, and ever-increasing debt, I found myself in the depths of a negative life cycle. I was stuck in a rut. Something was trying to tell me to snap out of it for a good few years. Being strapped to a heart monitor from excessive drinking wasn't enough, a near fatal car crash wasn't enough. It wasn't until I nearly lost my leg in a football accident that I finally decided enough was enough, and I finally acknowledged the fact that my life was in a bad place. I decided – no more negative relationships, no more overspending, no more unhealthy habits, no more dead-end jobs, and no more unhappiness. It was time to change.

Harnessing my amazing new energy, a Master's Degree in Psychology, and an obsession with studying human potential, I began developing a collection of techniques to turn every area of my life around. I've noticed a huge improvement in every area of my life from my confidence to my career, and even the way people behave towards me. Everything that I've learned and applied in my life, and other people's lives, the stuff that really works is the information you are about to read!

Two years, 300+ books, hundreds of seminars and webinars and practical application later, I am now crystal clear on my mission in life. My purpose in life and the aim of this book is to help you to realise how much health, happiness and success you have stored within you and show you how to release it.

I am still in the early stages of the journey of self-improvement and I want you to know that only three years ago I had all the same negative feelings and doubts that you have. It is exciting to think you can create your dream life though, isn't it? The best thing that I ever did was to jump in and go for it. You can do the same.

As you read on I want you to get in touch with the part of yourself that comes alive when you go to see a movie and you let your imagination run wild. I encourage you to do this because, at times, some of the things that I ask you to do may seem a little 'out-there' but with me as your guide you are going to follow my instructions and re-programme your mind for a whole new positive life!

THE RUT BUSTER SYSTEM™

> *"What the mind of man can conceive and believe, it can achieve"*
> Napoleon Hill

When I first decided to change my life, I remember just sitting for a moment and picturing in my mind what it could be like. I saw myself living up to my potential, living in a healthy body, with beautiful relationships, and with my dream career.

I'd like you to do the same now. Stop and vividly imagine in big, bright, high definition pictures how your life would look if everything was exactly the way you wanted it to be.

- What do you see?
- How do you feel?
- What do you hear?
- What does your body look like?
- How amazing is your career?
- What are your relationships like?
- How is your health?
- What are your finances like?

Notice how you feel better already. Your mind doesn't know the difference between a real experience and an imaginary one so the feelings are the same. As you use the strategies in this book you are going to make this vision a reality.

It is important that I make something crystal clear at this point. I am not into positive thinking for the sake of positive thinking. To paraphrase Anthony Robbins; I would not walk into your garden and say "there's no weeds, there's no weeds, there's no weeds!" We would get our hands in there and we would rip those weeds out! Exactly the same is true of your life and your mind. With this book as your guide you are going to remove the negativity from your life and your mind, and plant seeds of health, wealth and happiness. As these seeds start to grow, you will notice how amazed you are by the positive changes that start to happen in your life.

When I was designing the *Rut Buster System*, I had no idea what it would finally look like. I have come to realise that my mission is help you get to a point where you love your life and everything and everyone in it. You will start to love everything about your life as you make progress whilst reading this book, provided that you **decide** that your life is going to change and immediately take **action**.

The Captain & Crew of Your Marvellous Mind

> *"Whatever we plant in our subconscious mind and nourish with repetition and emotion will one day become a reality."*
>
> **Earl Nightingale**

To get the most out of the techniques in this book it is Vital that you imagine your mind being made up of two areas. One is your conscious mind and the other is your subconscious mind.

Your conscious mind is like the captain of your ship; whilst you are awake it is always analysing, critiquing and thinking 'logically'. If I ask you to stop right now and think of ten things you know about the USA, you literally have to stop and think about it using your conscious mind.

Your subconscious mind is like the crew of the ship, controlling all of your bodily functions, from your breathing to digesting your food. Your subconscious mind is where everything you have ever seen, heard, tasted, touched or smelled is stored; every memory and every experience. It is in the majesty of your subconscious mind where all of your problem-solving abilities lie as well as every ounce of your intelligence and creativity. If I ask you to stop right now and quickly put your right arm out to the side, you can do it immediately, without having to think of coordinating all of the 130 muscles involved. This is your subconscious mind taking control.

Your subconscious mind allows you to see things differently and solve your problems from a different angle. How many times have you gone to sleep with a problem and woken up with the answer? This is the phenomenon of the 'crew' of your subconscious mind, never sleeping and continuing to work on things whilst you are asleep.

Your subconscious mind is also where your mental habits live. We first learn to do something with our conscious mind and then it gets repeated and repeated until it is totally automatic and the conscious mind becomes less involved. The once new skill can be done without thinking. If you know how to drive a car, you will know exactly how this feels.

However, these skills are not limited to physical acts like driving a car. They can be skills like making ourselves feel bad, indecisiveness, getting stressed out, or being paralysed by fear of failure. They can also be helpful skills of feeling fantastic, motivated, confident and productive. You are going to replace all of the negative habits with positive ones through exciting, emotion-filled repetition. Please don't underestimate the power of repetition, because your subconscious mind will store that which is repeated by the conscious mind whether it's good or bad. The only reason you respond to your name automatically is because it is stored in your subconscious through constant repetition. You are going to use this technology by commanding and demanding your subconscious mind to deliver the body, finances, relationships and life that you want.

"You don't have to be great to start, but you have to start to be great."
Zig Ziglar

Decision

I have learned that you will never make positive changes in your life unless you truly **decide** to make that change, no matter what. When you have made a true decision, you have **decided** that it is going to happen for you regardless. That is why it is at the very top of *The Rut Buster System,* it's the very first step because unless you make that absolute decision, you will not make a positive change.

It all started with a decision for all great people; at a very young age Tiger Woods decided he was going to be the best golfer in the world. Donald Trump decided he was going to have a multi-billion dollar empire. Arnold Schwarzenegger decided that he was going to win Mr. Olympia (and indeed achieve many other things after that). I decided to write this book and when that that decision was made I had no intention of looking back.

As you read these words, decide that your life is going to be the way you want it to be in a very short space of time. Decide that as you practise the techniques in this book. Your life is going to improve day by day. Decide to permanently raise your standards in every area of your life because from this point on, anything below that standard is not acceptable! Using your body as an example, what would it be like if you had the standards of a professional athlete? Take a moment to imagine that you have these standards when it comes to the way you eat, exercise and take care of your body.

- What does your body look like?
- How do you feel?
- What are people saying to you about your body?

It is easy to see that **deciding** to permanently raise your standards can have a very profound effect on your life in a very short space of time.

STOP AND WRITE IT DOWN

There are going to be various times in this book when I ask you to stop and write something down. This serves two purposes. Firstly it will make the reading experience easier and you will stay focused. Secondly, writing things down imprints the ideas into your subconscious. Let's start with a quick exercise now:

Write down an area of your life in which you are going to permanently raise your standards.

How it will feel to be living with this new high standard?

Role Models

> "A role model is a mentor, someone you can learn from on a daily basis."
>
> **Denzel Washington**

Finding people who have already achieved the result that you want to achieve can cut the time it takes to achieve your goals or your dream life in half! Why would you want to learn from years and years of your own mistakes when you can learn from other people's mistakes? When I first discovered this idea I really started to love it. There are books written, videos recorded, and classes taught that are very affordable and readily available from people who have already done what you are trying to do! Why not just do what they did; it seemed to work didn't it? How many musical performers have dance moves that look a lot like Michael Jackson's? The answer is a lot, because he revolutionised performing and got such phenomenal feedback for his dancing it was inevitable that others would mimic his style.

Adopt the mindset and take the **action** of the people you'd love to be like and great things are about to happen in your life. Learn about how they think. If they have written books, read them. Find out how they got that body, or made that business work, or achieved their goals, and you can do the same. It would be great to get the same results in life as your heroes, wouldn't it?

Role models can also help you to realise that it's possible. If they can do it, you can do it! You will see the story of Roger Bannister as a metaphor for this idea everywhere but it is such a startling illustration of the phenomenon that it has to be mentioned here as well.

Scientists and other experts used to say that running the four-minute mile was not only dangerous but impossible. In the 1940's the record for running the mile stood at 4:01 and people started to believe that the human body had reached its limit. In 1954 Roger Bannister broke the four-minute barrier. Within six weeks someone else had done it. Now over a thousand people have done it – including high school kids! What changed? First and foremost, Bannister had to believe it was possible; he was repeating the images in his mind of actually achieving the feat. Once this vision became a reality for him it became obvious to everybody else that it was *possible*. The commonly held belief about running the four-minute mile had been irrevocably broken, and there was a role model who had shown the way.

I'd be honoured if you would let me be your mentor to turn your life around and escape your rut. I can help you to have a great life now and in the future. All I ask is that you continue to believe, and to keep a laser-focus on improving your life because you'll realise as you read these pages what you focus on expands.

Pick someone who has characteristics that you admire and would love to emulate. Now picture this person in your mind, doing the things that you admire them for. How do they move? How do they breathe? How do they think? What do they see? What do they hear?

Now imagine stepping into their body and notice how great it feels to merge all of your amazing characteristics with theirs. Feel yourself doing the things that they do and notice how you grow in confidence as you realise you can be just as great as they are.

STOP AND WRITE IT DOWN

What is it about them that you admire?

What are the best ways for you to learn how to do what they do so well?

Periodically you'll see the words *Take a Break*, just like the ones below. I have done a lot of reading over the past five years and I know how difficult it can be to hold concentration for long periods of time. So when you see *Take a Break,* jump up, have a stretch, have a glass of water, watch your favourite funny video, or listen to your favourite song. Do whatever you have to do to relax, refocus and be ready to get going again. So, give it a go now.

Beliefs

> *"If you don't change your beliefs, your life will be like this forever. Is that good news?"*
>
> **W. Maugham**

It is your beliefs that can hold you down, keep you where you are, and stop you from even attempting to improve your life. How often do you hear people say things like "I've tried everything to lose weight" or "No matter what I try, I just can't get out of debt"? Do you think that those people have really tried *everything* to lose weight or get out of debt? Of course they haven't. The chances are they have tried three or four things that didn't work for them, and then gave up. As a result they have started to believe that this is true for them. If you hold on to this type of belief your mind will do whatever it takes to prove itself right, and you'll stay stuck for the rest of your life.

However, beliefs can build us up and take us to new heights that we could previously have only imagined. Imagine you decided to believe that from this moment on you were destined to live beyond 100 years of age and be in amazing, vibrant shape deep into your old age? How would your day-to-day living change? Would you eat well? Would you exercise? Would you relax more often? Again, your mind would do everything to prove itself right in line with this belief.

The challenge is that beliefs are merely how you interpret an event and if these events are misinterpreted then we could potentially have a disempowering belief that negatively impacts our life. For example, take two people who are bullied from a young age in school. How is that one becomes a bully and one becomes a charitable, 'people' person? The answer is clear, it is not what happens to us; it is our interpretation and response to what happens that makes the difference.

When I decided that I was going to run a half marathon for Cancer Research I had to tear down some disempowering beliefs. I had been told all my life that my asthma was negatively impacting my cardiovascular fitness and more recently that the titanium rod and screws in my leg would mean I couldn't run more than a mile on a hard surface. I had fallen victim to other people's opinions as opposed to creating my own life. I had made other people's opinions my beliefs and this is very easily done if you do not stand guard at the door of your mind. Take note of the words of motivational speaker Les Brown: "Someone's opinion of you does not have to become your reality".

How do you break down a disempowering belief and replace it with an empowering one? **Change the picture you're holding in your mind.** I realised that when I believed that I couldn't run long distances I was holding pictures in my mind of me doubled over in pain with my leg and struggling to breathe. I began training my mind to see myself crossing the finishing line feeling healthy, happy, proud and in control. I did this every day until my mind accepted it as reality and I believed that it could be done.

Everything that was ever created, everything that you see around you right now, including this book, began as a picture in someone's mind.

STOP AND WRITE IT DOWN

Write down *everything* that you believe about life, other people, your happiness, motivation, health, body, money, relationships, career and your future.

STOP AND WRITE IT DOWN

Now go back and divide the beliefs into *beliefs that help* me and *beliefs that hurt* me. With the beliefs that help you I want you to make them even stronger and write them down in an improved way. For example: "I believe that people like me because I am friendly" could become "I am totally certain that people love me because I am loving, caring and generous in every relationship I create." Re-write them below.

STOP AND WRITE IT DOWN

Next, with the beliefs that hurt you, it is beneficial to attach enough emotional pain from within: picture how believing it all these years has had a negative impact on your life. Ask how it is negatively impacting your life right now. Allow yourself to realise the fact that you will not have the future that you desire if you continue to believe it. You can now turn them into their absolute opposite. For example: "I can't get the body I want because of my genetics" could become "I am totally certain that by following the right nutrition and exercise program I can get the body of my dreams".

Decide that you are no longer willing to hold on to the beliefs that hurt you and you are only ever going to repeat and hold in your mind beliefs that help you. With practice this will change your life.

You are about to realise that no one can tell you what something means and you can choose to believe whatever you want, can't you? Over time, you will notice that you become focused on solutions to problems, rather than the problems themselves.

Living from this place of strength means that you are big enough to deal with whatever comes your way. You will start to take **action** on the things you want from life because you now believe it's possible. This means that you have escaped your rut already because you now believe that everything is happening in your favour and it is all part of the process. Believe that small improvements every single day are inevitable, and this will ultimately make your life the way you want it to be.

Habits

> *"Successful people are simply those with successful habits."*

Brian Tracy

The results that we get in our lives are largely dictated by our habits. Think about it: if you don't eat or drink too many sugary substances and clean and floss your teeth every day, the result is that you have got healthy, bright, white teeth. If you don't clean and floss your teeth every day the result is that your teeth have cavities and are rotting.

It is absolutely essential that, if we want the successful result, we have the successful habits to create it. How often do you hear people say things like "I need to lose weight" and then you see those people eating fatty unhealthy foods every day? The result you want - a healthy great looking body - is impossible when the eating habits are unhealthy.

What habits can you form that will accelerate your progress? This is where it all started for me and I soon realised that one good habit is like a magnet for another, and soon you'll be doing healthy, happy, empowering things every day.

A way to fast track this is to find a role model and ask them what their habits are, and how they've achieved the result that you want, and then you can replicate those habits. Within the following chapters I'll reveal the habits that have worked for me in each area of my life and ultimately, how easy it is to make the change.

STOP AND WRITE IT DOWN

Understand that you are not a robot. You are a magnificent human being and you can take control of your daily actions. Have some fun now and laugh as you write down and realise some things that you do on a regular basis that you know are not good for you, but you still do without thinking.

Decide that from now on you are going to consciously take control of the things that you do on a daily basis until the things that you do on autopilot contribute directly to you having a better life. The bonus to this lifestyle is that treats mean so much more. Let's say you were improving your health and you decided to stop eating chocolate every day without thinking. How much more fulfilling would it be those one or two times a month when you treated yourself to a bar of chocolate, knowing you are living in a healthy, great looking body?

Discipline

> *"To enjoy good health, to bring true happiness to one's family, to bring peace to all, one must first discipline and control one's own mind."*
>
> **Buddha**

The concept of discipline is very easy to grasp and everything that you are about to read you probably already know but you don't truly *know it* unless you *live it!*

To live with true discipline you have to have taken the first step and **decided** to get a particular result. If you have made a true decision then the discipline will automatically follow. Just like the rocket that uses 80% of its fuel to leave planet Earth, you will require the highest levels of discipline for the first ten to twenty days after you have decided to make change. Have the discipline to follow this book through to the end and positively change your life and you will have started to build the habit of being disciplined. Discipline builds more discipline. Simple concept, isn't it?

STOP AND WRITE IT DOWN

What does discipline mean to you, and how can you apply this in your life?

Knowledge

> *"Knowledge is only potential power until it comes into the hands of someone who knows how to get himself to take effective action."*
>
> **Anthony Robbins**

I believe that we should always be on a continuous quest for knowledge. However, why is it that there are so many people who have so much knowledge, yet they do not have the life that you would expect them to have? I'll give you a personal example. For many years I was repeatedly told that eating and drinking a lot of dairy was having a negative effect on my asthma, but why did I keep consuming it? Knowledge is absolutely worthless unless acted upon!

- 65% of people reading this book will read some or most of it and then do absolutely nothing.
- 30% of people will read it and then make positive changes for a week or two and then go backwards.
- 5% of people will read the information in this book and then take persistent, continuous **action** on it for the rest of their lives and ultimately end up living the life they desire.

I don't give you those statistics to be negative, they are just the reality. The funny thing is, I have been part of all three groups, but I've now realised that life can be a lot more fun and you can make faster progress if you are part of the 5%. Decide to be part of the 5% right now and make rapid progress.

The knowledge about what you want to achieve will always be available. However, the decision to act on the knowledge can only come from you.

STOP AND WRITE IT DOWN

What knowledge do you most need to acquire?

Goals

Goal setting can get you what you want! It's as simple as that. The pursuit of worthy goals will transform you into a person that you had no idea you were capable of becoming!

Goals really have changed my life and I have achieved things I had no idea I was capable of. I have certainly become a person that I had no idea that I could be. I was shocked to learn that only 20% of people actually set goals and only 6% of people ever achieve their goals.

I have personally used an almost obsessive study of human potential, success and personal development literature to devise what I believe to be the most effective way to set goals. I call it *The 4-Wheel Drive Method*[TM].

There are 4 'W's' in the *The 4-Wheel Drive Method*[TM] that represent the wheels on a 4x4 vehicle and, just like a 4x4 vehicle, when you have all of these wheels working together to help you set and achieve goals, no terrain is too difficult. At the moment you may have goals that are okay if all is going well, but what if you have to 'go off road' and tackle some tough situations? The *The 4-Wheel Drive Method*[TM] will take care of that for you.

THE FOUR W'S

1. **W**hat do I want, exactly?
2. **W**hy exactly do I want it?
3. **W**hen exactly do I want it by?
4. **W**hat must I do to get it?

1. **What do I want, exactly?**

If you don't define what it is that you want, exactly, then your mind has no idea how to get it. If you wanted to drive to your hotel in Paris from London, would you find the exact address of the hotel or would you just type 'France' into the satellite navigation system? Your brain works the same way; it needs to know exactly where you want to go. A lot of the time people are setting loose goals and achieving them. How often have you heard someone say "I want to lose some weight" and when they only lose a pound they are disappointed. How can they be disappointed when they have achieved their goal!?

2. Why exactly do I want it?

You need to know why you want to achieve whatever it is that you want to achieve, and it has to be powerful enough to get you to do the things that you have to do even when you don't feel like doing them. Let's say that you wanted to lose five pounds of body fat. If the 'Why' was "So I can fit into my birthday dress" this may create some leverage, but it is only likely to be short term, and you will probably put the weight back on after your birthday. What if the 'Why' was more powerful? "So I can be the best version of myself humanly possible, remaining healthy, vibrant and energetic every single day, enabling me to do more, be more and have more. Giving me more years with my children, grandchildren and great grandchildren and inspiring them along the way"?

Do you see how this 'Why' is far more likely to create leverage and lead to lasting change?

3. When exactly do I want it by?

Your brain needs an exact date to get you to take enough action at the right times. To use the holiday analogy again, imagine you said: "We're going on holiday next summer." and left it at that. How would you know when to go shopping for the items you needed? How would you know when to pack? The answer is simply that you wouldn't! That is why the reality is you'd be better saying something like: "We're going to Madrid on the 17th July 2014". Your brain would know that it has to do everything that it needs to in preparation for the trip. Goals are the same.

4. What must I do to get it?

This wheel has the most freedom out of all of the wheels because you may not know everything that you have to do to achieve the goals, but it will be vital for you to take massive action and start as soon as possible! It is important that you work out what you are going to do first and find a plan, a mentor or a strategy, but the most important thing is to get moving!

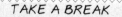

TAKE A BREAK

Putting it all Together

Once you have gone through the above process of creating a goal you are left with something that should be phrased like the example that follows. Note the tense in which it is written – it's as if it's already happened and is a reality. This provokes positive feelings of it already being achieved and magnetises the subconscious mind to achieve everything you'll need to do to attain the goal. Once you have all of your goals written out in this way it is important to review them at least once a day. I will go into detail on how to do this a little later.

Here is a goal that I recently achieved that will show you how it can be phrased. It was written on December 10th, 2012.

> *"It is October 6th 2013 and I am so happy and grateful that I easily completed the Cardiff half marathon in less than two and a half hours in honour of my dear Grandfather, and in support of Cancer Research UK. This is an amazing achievement for me and it serves as a signpost in my life that I am over the broken leg that I suffered, and that I no longer suffer from asthma. I feel healthy, vibrant and energised by the achievement, and it has given me an insight into how I can achieve whatever I put my mind to."*

I completed the race on October 6th, 2013 in a time of 2 hours and 14 minutes.

STOP AND WRITE IT DOWN

Now, write a specific goal of your own.

Physiology, Focus & Mind Images

> *"The only limits in life are the ones we impose on ourselves"*
> **Bob Proctor**

It is quite possible that if you are feeling down and de-motivated about life on a regular basis then you are *making yourself* feel that way.

Think for a moment of the golfer who, straight after he hits the poor shot, immediately and almost proudly states "I knew that I was going to put that in the water!" How did they know? Because as they gingerly approached the ball, they felt unhappy about hitting the shot and they watched it go in the water in their mind before they even swung the club.

The chain of negative processes can then continue when we routinely speak to ourselves in a way that we would never do to anybody else! We say things like: "You are such an idiot!" or "Why can't you do anything right?" It is easy to see how negative states are pretty much guaranteed if we approach life and situations like this on a regular basis.

So what are you supposed to do about this? How can you choose to be happy and to control your state? It is very simple, take conscious control over the most powerful computer in the universe, your mind, and make it a habit to take control of the way you move, the images you make in your mind, and the way you talk to yourself.

You could start by making a conscious, deliberate, determined effort to hold yourself as if you were the happiest person in the world and your biochemistry will follow suit. How would you be holding your body if you were 100% confident in yourself, with the body of your dreams, and financially free? Where would your shoulders be? Where would your head be? How would you be breathing?

You can start moving like this *right now*. Start conducting yourself as if all of your goals had already been achieved. Somebody who is a happy success, like Richard Branson for example, moves his body in a very different way to someone who is depressed. **Decide** that you are no longer willing to hold yourself in that timid, depressed position ever again. The minute you start to feel your shoulders or head start to drop, take action immediately and readjust your body. Move, dance, jump up and down; do whatever it takes to change your physiology, no matter how silly it feels, because if you don't you could be on a downward spiral of feeling extremely negative.

When you're walking around with your shoulders back, chest up and head up, your mind feels like you are in control and it believes that you are the type of person who can go out and achieve your goals.

Emotion is created by motion. It is vital that you take this on board. Think about it for a moment - have you ever been jumping up and down with a huge smile on your face and felt the feeling of sadness at the same time? What about when your favourite sports team has scored, how do you move your body?

If you are making yourself feel down you are probably not just holding yourself in a negative way. You are also holding negative pictures in your mind and focusing on the wrong things by asking yourself disempowering questions.

I'd like you to think of the worst movie you have watched. Would you watch it again? Probably not. So why is it that when something bad happens to us we relive it, and watch it, and relive it, and watch it, over and over again? Just wipe the screen of your mind and choose to hold an image in mind that makes you feel good instead.

Finally, be extra vigilant about what you are saying to yourself. Successful entrepreneur, John Assaraf, said "Be very careful what you say to yourself, someone important is listening... you!" How many of us know someone who says things like "These things always happen to me" or "I'm so unlucky"? We have to be very careful about what we say becoming a self-fulfilling prophecy. Unless of course you say "I'm always happy, healthy and confident!"

I am very passionate about you taking **action** to take control of your state, because it is something that will improve the quality of your life *straight away*. With practice, if you notice yourself slipping into a negative physiology with negative mind images and poor self-talk, you'll be able to take control straight away.

TAKE A BREAK

Action, Persistence, & New Strategy

> *"Our greatest weakness lies in giving up. The most certain way to succeed is to try one more time."*
>
> **Thomas Edison**

When you have your new belief that you can achieve anything that you want to achieve, it is imperative that you take constant action towards making your dreams become a reality.

A lot of people will talk about visualising their goals and holding pictures in their mind, and that is crucial, but what if you visualised yourself as owning a Fortune-500 company but then you sat around on the couch all day, watching TV? It just wouldn't happen.

Whatever you decide to achieve throughout the course of this book, make sure that you take the action required to make it happen, otherwise all of the mind-set improvement will just be a waste of time.

Be aware of the fact that it is rare for huge success to just fall into your lap. A certain amount of persistence is required. Keep going, keep going and keep going until you get there. As I sit and write this book I have not achieved my dream life yet. Yes, it has drastically improved, but there are still many dreams to make a reality. The great thing about being persistent is you know that you're going to achieve your goals because you're not going to stop until you do.

You have to be careful not to persist in doing things that have been proven not to work. Find new strategies until your goal is achieved.

STOP AND WRITE IT DOWN

What strategies are you going to employ to stay on track?

A Contract with Yourself

It is time to imprint your intentions onto your subconscious mind by signing your name to a declaration that states you are committed to improving your life:

I,

... hereby commit to the decision I have made to improve my life. I will only entertain beliefs that help me. My habits will be habits that contribute directly to my health, wealth and happiness. I will have fun being disciplined in every area of my life. I will be on a constant quest for knowledge. I will set and achieve goals that get me excited every day. I will use my body, mind and inner voice to create amazing feelings and emotions every day. I will take action every day towards achieving my goals and I will be persistent on my journey to finding the strategies that will make my dreams become a reality.

Signed

Dated

Congratulations, and thank you for coming this far, you now understand the tools you need to turn your life around.
As you improve every area of your life you will notice how each part of *The Rut Buster System* is involved at different times.
Let's have some fun and make your dreams a reality...

- PART 1 -
CHANGE YOURSELF

> *"Most folks are as happy as they make up their minds to be."*
> Abraham Lincoln

The cars, the clothes, the holiday homes,
This man had it all.
He spent his life in party mode,
It seemed just like a ball!

He had a massive business,
A trophy wife as well,
Famous for his intellect
But for him, every day was hell.

It all became too much,
He had nowhere else to turn
There was one crucial secret,
That he didn't get to learn.

His success was plain for all to see,
The champagne was always swishing,
But instead of what he had
He focused on what was missing...

Jermaine Harris

The Happiness Cycle

What is the key to happiness? It's not money, otherwise all millionaires would be happy. It's not having a great body, otherwise all professional athletes would be happy. It's not being in a relationship, otherwise all married people would be happy. It's not having a 'good job', otherwise all doctors and lawyers would be happy. So what the heck is it? I believe that two of the primary keys to happiness are *being happy now* by focusing on what you have and *making constant progress*.

It has become so obvious to me over the years that it is not what happens to us that determines whether we are happy or not. It is how we respond to what happens. That is why the very first

33

part of this book addresses happiness, because without **deciding** to be happy first, success in any other area of life becomes empty.

IT'S NOT THE WAY IT'S 'SUPPOSED' TO BE

How is it that two women can weigh 250 pounds and one is depressed and feels ugly while the other feels like she is sexy and working it? It is because the one who feels depressed has a picture in her mind of what she *should* look like, and it is not the way she is right now. This inevitably means that she will feel unhappy. The woman who feels sexy also has a picture in her mind of what sexy should look like and she looks exactly like that, so she is happy.

This is true across all areas of life. If you took one of the world's wealthiest billionaires and made him or her merely a millionaire overnight they would be totally devastated. However, if I made you a millionaire overnight you'd probably be very happy, wouldn't you?

The Danger of *When*

> *"Happiness doesn't depend on any external conditions; it is governed by our mental attitude."*
> **Dale Carnegie**

One of the first things that I discovered and now teach is never to use the phrase "I'll be happy when..." You have either said, or heard people say, at least one of these things: "I'll be happy when I get more money", "I'll be happy when I lose some weight", or "I'll be happy when I meet someone". Whenever you are saying "I'll be happy when..." you are training yourself to base your happiness on things that are coming rather than things that you have at the moment. This means you will never be happy. As bleak as that may sound, you can make an immediate change just by changing one word in the sentence...

STOP AND WRITE IT DOWN

Complete the sentences that follow with as many things as you can. Let everything flow out of you. From the roof over your head, to your ability to see, include everything.

I am happy because

I am happy because

I am happy because

I am happy because

I am happy because

I am happy because

I am happy because

I am happy because

I am happy because

I am happy because

You have just written down 10 reasons as to why you are happy right now. You have reasons to be happy every day. Perhaps you just don't focus on them. By focusing on the sentence "I am happy because…" every day, you will train your brain to look for reasons to be happy right now. Once you start being happy right now you are no longer chasing happiness because you think you want certain things in your life. If you start your quest for new challenges and things from a place of being already happy, you are no longer attempting to simply fill a void.

Move to the Positive Side of the Street

> *"Once you replace negative thoughts with positive ones,*
> *you'll start having positive results."*
> **Willie Nelson**

I can promise you right now that your life will never be the same again when you realise that No one can control what you think. It may take a little discipline and persistence at first but, when you take responsibility for your happiness and control the images and sounds that are going on in your mind, happiness is inevitable.

If I asked you to "Think of a feather right now", you don't think the letters F-E-A-T-H-E-R. You have a picture of a feather on the screen of your mind. Realising that you have control of this is incredible. Try this now and let the images come in to your mind. Think of a black cat, now think of a polar bear, now think of a sandy desert… Amazing, isn't it? The image on the screen of your mind actually changes. Now think about someone you love with all your heart, make the picture big, bright and detailed. Allow a smile to dance into your eyes and then smile a big smile as you think about them.

The thought of this person makes you feel happy, doesn't it? Wouldn't it be marvellous if you had five or six thoughts like this that you could picture in your mind that would make you feel happy at any given moment? The good news is you can control the images in your mind, you have just done it with cats and polar bears. So you can think about things that make you smile whenever you want to.

{ STOP AND WRITE IT DOWN }

Describe in detail the picture you see in your mind of five people or things in your life that make you happy just by thinking about them.

1

2

3

4

5

The real magic occurs when you develop the discipline to realise that you are having a down moment and then picture the things that you have just written down to bring yourself back into a happy state. As you do this more and more, you will find yourself flicking through your 'happiness catalogue' automatically. Persist with this and I promise you that it will change your life, because you will have taken control of your moment-to-moment happiness, which I believe is the greatest success of all.

SEE IT AS IT IS, BUT NOT WORSE!

Each and every one of us has been hit by life. Of course we have. We've been left by people we love when we've done everything right, bills we haven't been able to pay on time, jobs that we have lost, loved ones who have passed away. It really does feel like we can't make it through the day sometimes, but we usually do.

We (myself included) may fall into the trap of making the situation seem totally dire with an inevitable, catastrophic ending. However, 99% of these catastrophes never arise. I know people who have been struggling to pay a mortgage payment and all of a sudden they are jumping all the way into predicting the loss of the house. The fascinating thing is that they are still living in the same house years later. What's happening here? They are getting themselves consistently worked up about a challenge they have been able to overcome again and again, and yet they still continue to talk about the worst case scenario.

It is essential that you develop the skill of immediately focusing on solutions to your current challenge and not wasting precious mental energy imagining all of the bigger challenges that could result from the situation that you are facing right now.

STOP AND WRITE IT DOWN

Think about a challenge you are facing in your life right now and answer the following, solution-focused questions (it may be difficult at first, but keep asking yourself the questions and your mind will be compelled to give you an answer):

What is the <u>best</u> thing about this situation?

What is not perfect yet?

What am I willing to do to improve the situation?

What am I no longer willing to do that is keeping me in this situation?

What is the best way for me to have fun along the way as I do everything required for me to improve the situation?

TAKE A BREAK

Help Someone Else

> *"There is no exercise better for the heart than reaching down and lifting people up."*
> **John Holmes**

Whatever situation you are in, there is someone not too far away from you who is worse off than you are. Find someone or a group of people who are in a worse situation than you are and help them in whatever way that you can. Kindness is not a one-way street. Have you noticed that every time you do something that makes someone feel good, you feel good as well?

Helping someone else is such a wonderful way to improve someone else's life, and to help you in the process. This can almost become a positive addiction, because any pain you are experiencing begins to fade away as you ease someone else's. You will feel happy in the knowledge that you have made a difference in someone else's life and your focus will be away from your own struggles.

TURN THAT FROWN UPSIDE DOWN

I know that it sounds like a cliché but just smiling can have a seriously dramatic effect on making you feel happier. You can couple this with changing the way you hold your body and the way you use your voice. Have you ever experienced a person with their head held high, their chest up and their shoulders back with a huge smile on their face frantically telling you how down in the dumps they are? I didn't think so. When people are telling you how sad they are, their shoulders are hunched, their head is down, their facial expression is glum and they are speaking slowly because they know that *saying* what is wrong is even more difficult.

The body and mind are constantly linked and one is always affecting the other. What if we could use this to our advantage? Some people seem to accept that you can think yourself ill, but that it's stupid to believe you can think yourself well. You can make amazing improvements in the way that you feel by radically changing your body. The best thing about this is that you can catch it early. The minute that you find yourself sitting or standing in a negative way, you can immediately take action.

You can put a big smile on your face, throw your shoulders back and look up, and your mind is wired to not allow you to feel depressed in this state. You'll notice how much better you feel. This is another process where you have to re-train your mind and body and, believe me, the persistence and discipline will pay off because you will be in charge of the way that you feel.

WORDS ARE POWERFUL

What you say out loud and in your head will expand in your life. The more you talk about a thing, the more you are attracting it into your life. Think about this for a moment. Do the people who always talk about debt quickly get out of debt? Do the people who always talk about being overweight quickly get the body they want? Do the people who moan about their children's behaviour quickly control it? Do the people who always say they are unhappy quickly get happy?

Now that you have **decided to be happy,** and you are serious about it, you are going to have to start taking control of the things you say. You have to decide to speak well of yourself and stop unnecessarily putting yourself down. You are not pretending to be perfect, you are simply realising that it cannot possibly be helpful to allow the sound of moaning about your job, family, friends, and everything else to vibrate through your body.

When we think about what we have learned about the subconscious mind this makes taking control of the words that we are using even more important. The words that we are saying with emotion are always finding their way into our subconscious and staying there and ultimately becoming part of our character.

You are probably trying to improve your life, right? You're trying to lose weight, you're trying to improve your finances and you're trying to be happy. Imagine for a moment what life would be like if you stopped 'trying' to do things and you just did them. If you are persistent and disciplined with yourself to eliminate the word *try* from your vocabulary then you will train your mind to be someone who **decides** to do something and then does it.

PROGRESS, PROGRESS, PROGRESS

To be happy as often as possible I truly believe that it is important to commit to making constant progress. No matter what endeavour you are involved with, from sport to business, you have to keep improving to keep up. Making constant progress is an amazing vehicle for happiness. I often hear people say things like "Why does Oprah keep working, surely she has enough money?" Oprah is clearly committed to constantly making progress. She reaches more and more people every year, and is always expanding on her ideas to serve people in more abundant and diverse ways.

I have worked with professional athletes to make sure that they set goals for after their retirement, otherwise they are setting themselves up for unhappiness. They have to have something to focus on that they can make progress towards. The same is true for you, and this is another reason why goals are so important.

WIN THE DAY

You don't have to achieve some huge 90-day goal to be making progress. Commit to making the most of any given 24-hour period. Do a little more than you did yesterday. If you went for a 15-minute walk around the block yesterday and you go for a 16-minute walk today, you have made progress.

Keep score of everything that you do so you can track your progress. Then you will always be able to see how far you have come, as opposed to how far you still have to go.

FUTURE TRUTH

Have you ever told someone with absolute authority that you were going to achieve some goal or dream, only for them to kill your enthusiasm by saying something like "Don't lie to yourself."

What if you were just telling the truth in advance?

Every so often, I am going to ask you to stand up, put your hand on your heart and *tell the truth in advance*. I call these 'Future Truths'. You are going to say each future truth with such passion and enthusiasm (not necessarily aloud) that it vibrates through your whole body. You are going to hold your body in a way that you would be holding it if it was absolute reality.

WARNING: If you don't want to improve your life then you don't have to do this. It may feel weird, but do it on your own and you don't have to worry about what anybody thinks because they never need to know. Here is your first one.

"I am so happy and grateful for everything that I have right now. I choose to be happy because I am always in control of what I focus on."

Massive Motivation – You *can* be Bothered

How do you get motivated?
The young apprentice asked.
"Ah this is a crucial lesson,
For your goals to be surpassed!"

I'll ask you a question,
As you've started aiming higher
What would you do if you woke up one night,
And your house was on fire?

Would you take some time to psyche yourself up
And wait for motivation to grow?
Or would you jump up out of bed,
Grab your family, take a deep breath and go?

People wait for January,
Like motivation is a 'season'
But really and truly; like the fire
All you need is a big enough reason…

Jermaine Harris

A few weeks after I made my decision to turn my life around, I had hundreds of sheets of paper with notes about how to improve my life on them. I really wanted to get myself going and when I started to analyse the notes that I had on motivation it seemed that setting goals was something that kept coming up.

I was constantly reading about how the most motivated people in the world were people who set goals, and impressive goals at that. Think about it, does the British runner, Mo Farah, run over one hundred miles per week because he is just going through the motions or does he do it because he has the goal of winning Olympic medals?

Setting goals is the one thing that got me going, and setting and pursuing goals still gets me motivated to such extreme levels that people think that there's something wrong with me.

43

Everything about me as a person – my health, my income, my contribution to society, my personality, and my happiness have drastically improved because I have mastered the art of motivation through goal setting.

As you read the following chapters it is important that you follow the *The 4-Wheel Drive Method*^{TM}, for goal setting and set goals in each area of your life. When you have a goal for each area of your life and you take action on them all every single day, you'll notice everything in your life starts to improve.

BIG DREAMS = BIG MOTIVATION

> *"All our dreams can come true, if we have the courage to pursue them."*
> **Walt Disney**

Think of goals in three categories:

1. Goals you *know* you can achieve
2. Goals you *think* you can achieve and
3. Goals you actually *want* to achieve.

Type 1 goals and Type 2 goals create no leverage or inspiration for you. They are exactly the type of goals that mean you have to read this chapter on motivation. Type 3 goals, however, inspire you to take action. They are so compelling that motivation is no longer an issue.

I'll give you an example: I used to have the goal of "being a life coach with 10 clients" (Type 1 goal, I knew I could do this). I then had the goal of "50 people have been through my life coaching program" (Type 2 goal, I thought I could this). At the time of writing my goal is now "to impact the lives of over 1,000,000 people globally through my books, products, seminars and speeches, (Type 3 goal - this is what I really want!). I don't need any outside inspiration any more. I know what I want, I truly believe that I can achieve it, and I have no idea how to do it right now, but that doesn't matter.

YOU ARE ALREADY A MASTER OF MOTIVATION!

You have already mastered motivation, you just don't realise it. A true mastery of motivation comes from being 100% committed to something. Do you need to watch a motivational video or listen to motivational music to wash yourself every day? Of course not. You are just 100% committed to being clean and hygienic. You just do it. What if you had this same approach to doing whatever it is you currently wish you were motivated to do?

It is absolutely crucial that you get in touch with what you are motivated to create in your life every day! This reprogramming process is amazing because I have realised over time that if you don't program yourself, you will be programmed by the environment and the people closest to you.

DO YOU HAVE A BIG ENOUGH REASON?

If you were in bed and you realised that your house was on fire would you roll over and have five more minutes sleep, or would you be motivated to jump out of bed and get yourself and your family to safety as quickly as possible? You would take immediate **action**, the reason being that if you didn't, you and your family would probably die.

The most important factor in being motivated to achieve anything is *Why?* Different things act as motivators for different people but we all have certain things that can get us to take action. With a bit of deep thought we can all come up with a compelling list of things to motivate ourselves. There are things like making a positive difference to the world, becoming financially free, and doing it for my family. When these are all aligned you'll quickly realise that you won't have to worry about being motivated ever again, because it is happening whether you feel motivated or not.

STOP AND WRITE IT DOWN

Pick something you want to achieve in your life and write down every reason you can think of as to why it has to happen for you.

Now close your eyes and picture how the 100% committed version of yourself operates. Feel how great it feels to be constantly taking action on your goals. As you do this, make sure you have a big smile on your face and notice how motivated you feel right now to finally make your life exactly what you want it to be.

CHASING GOOD FEELINGS AND ESCAPING BAD ONES

You know exactly what you want your ideal life to look like and yet you still don't take the action that would make it a reality. What keeps you from starting that new exercise regime? What stops you from acting on that business idea that you have had for as long as you can remember? Why haven't you started taking control of your finances?

You are 100% aware of the fact that taking these actions will improve your life on an *intellectual* level, so why don't you do it? It is because you believe that escaping the bad feelings associated with taking those actions is more important than the potential good feelings. What if you went through the physical pain and struggle of that difficult exercise regime only to put all the weight back on anyway? What if the business was a flop? What if you had to give up doing the things you love to do in order to sort your finances?

When I first encountered this idea, I became obsessed with discovering why people who were obviously experiencing bad feelings would carry on living in exactly the same way. It became apparent that these people simply weren't experiencing bad feelings that were intense enough to force them to make a change. If you have ever made a decision to finally lose weight, gain muscle or finally improve your health it was because you had so many intense bad feelings associated with how your body was looking that you simply were not willing to live like it anymore. It is quite simple when you think about it like this. What motivated you? You wanted to escape the bad feelings that being out of shape brought into your life, and you were chasing the good feelings that would come with looking and feeling good.

Understanding this linkage to our behaviour of seeking good feelings and avoiding bad feelings can help us to be motivated to do anything we want, or indeed de-motivate us from doing the things that do not help us.

I remember my mother telling me the story of the time she thought it would be cool to have a cigarette. At the time she was chasing the good feeling of being cool. Fortunately for her, my grandfather caught her in the act, and in his wisdom made her smoke the whole pack there and then. Although this may seem extreme it was certainly enough to make sure my mother never touched a cigarette ever again. For the rest of her life my mother

47

has been escaping the intense bad feelings of vomiting, and difficulty breathing that she had associated with smoking cigarettes.

Your life is about to totally change when you realise the power of this concept. The amazing thing about motivation is that you are clearly motivated to do some things in your life, but these things may not help you and may have a direct impact on your motivation to do other things. For example if you are motivated to stay up late every night, it is likely that you are not going to be motivated to get up early in the morning. It is vitally important that you address the things that you are motivated to do, but want to eliminate, as well as increasing your motivation to do the things that you know will improve your life. I used to be very motivated to go out on the weekends and spend more money than I earned on alcohol. I was chasing the good feelings of feeling free, of staying young, of living for the moment. I was also trying to escape the bad feelings of boredom, routine, and never enjoying myself.

STOP AND WRITE IT DOWN

Think of something that you seem very motivated to do that you know isn't good for your health, wealth or long-term happiness. Write down the good feelings you are trying to create by doing it and the bad feelings that you escape. Keep writing, allow every feeling to hit the page.

STOP AND WRITE IT DOWN

Now write down all of the intense bad feelings that could potentially happen if you keep engaging in this behaviour. For example, I wrote down several. I could have a stroke / heart attack or any other alcohol-induced illness. I would never fulfil my potential and die a nobody. I would be a disgrace to my family if I continued. Even as I write these words I am so grateful that I have escaped those bad feelings. You will too. Keep writing, let every feeling come out.

STOP AND WRITE IT DOWN

You can now pick something positive that you want to be motivated to do. Write down all of the amazing feelings that you will create for yourself by **taking this action,** and write down all of the bad feelings you will be escaping. This will be twice as powerful if you can utilise the same feelings that you were chasing and escaping before. As an example, you'll remember that I wanted to feel I was free, staying young, and like I was living for the moment, and that I didn't want to feel boring, stuck in a routine and never enjoying myself. I have used these feelings to my advantage because I am now extremely motivated to be a global name in the field of personal development and travel the world, spreading my message. Why? Because I know that I'll feel free, young and in the moment as I live this lifestyle, and I certainly won't find it boring. I won't be stuck in a routine and I'll certainly be enjoying myself. Have some fun with this, write as much as you can and you'll notice how great it feels to realise you can get the same feelings doing positive things.

Awareness and repetition are very important when it comes to making this work for you. When you feel yourself wanting to break your new eating habits and just go on a binge, be aware of the fact that you are just chasing a good feeling. Then, stop and picture the pain of being overweight again and all of the illnesses that will come your way if you eat like this. It is about thinking about the long-term feelings. Do you think as many double cheeseburgers would be eaten if, three seconds after you ate one, you gained twenty pounds and had a heart attack?

THAT LITTLE VOICE IN YOUR HEAD

You go to bed motivated and totally ready for tomorrow. You know that you are going to get up early, go to the gym and start the day with astounding momentum. You go to sleep safe in the knowledge that tomorrow is going to be a day full of motivation. The next morning your alarm goes off and you immediately hear words like "Really? It can't be time to get up already", " I'll hit snooze, 5 more minutes won't hurt", "I tell you what, you can start that new routine tomorrow". What happened?

That wasn't you speaking, it was your little voice. Your little voice can be a troublemaker, while it does only want to protect you, it really can sabotage you and drain you of all your motivation. You probably hear that little voice in your head every day in many different situations. "You can't do that." "That's too difficult." "Don't ask her on a date, she might say no." You may have even heard it as you're reading this book. "That wouldn't work for me." "What is this nonsense?" It is trying to protect you through a fear of things going wrong if you try to improve, and it knows that you are safe where you are.

The most reassuring realisation is that this voice isn't you! It is your conditioned mind that may have been negatively programmed at some point in your past. The chances are that it will always be there, but it is up to you how you respond to it and how you view it.

Think of something that your little voice says to you regularly – it will be things like "You can never lose weight", "You can't start a business", or "You'll always be single". Hear it saying those words to you now. Where in your head is it? What does it sound like? Is it speaking fast or slow? Loudly or quietly? Now picture the same voice talking out of your belly button in a silly way like *Donald Duck,* or in a silly accent. Notice how you have control over it and realise it isn't as threatening now.

One of the most powerful things that I did when I was taking control of the conversation in my head was to visualise my little voice and draw what he looked like. He turned out to be this tiny stick man with a speech bubble coming out of his mouth and scraggly hair. After I did this I realised that I had a big voice as well, the voice that tells you that you *can* do things, and knows that it is your duty to create the best life possible even if it does mean some persistence and a few calculated risks. I then visualised my big voice and in the true unpredictable fashion of the human mind it turned out to be champion bodybuilder Kai Greene. If you don't know who Kai Greene is, he is a giant of a man with huge muscles in every area of his body. Now, if a battle takes place in my head between the "You can't" of the little voice and the "You can" of the big voice, Kai Greene is going to dominate a little stick man every day of the week!

STOP AND WRITE IT DOWN

Take the time to visualise, and then draw, what your little voice looks like with a speech bubble saying something it usually says to de-motivate you. Then visualise and draw your big voice with a bigger speech bubble, powerfully saying the opposite, motivating words.

Whenever you notice yourself feeling de-motivated by the things you are saying to yourself, have the discipline to realise that it isn't you and it is that harmless little drawing. Visualise your big voice taking control and motivating you to take **action.**

Be persistent with this and soon you will notice that your big voice is running the show and you will be on a motivated fast track to achieving your goals. Which is what you want, right?

MOTIVATION IS JUST A FEELING

The interesting thing about motivation is it is just a feeling, like happiness or sadness. So it's important that you do that little bit extra every day to create the *feeling* of motivation. I can't tell you what that is for you, but you will already know.

I like to watch motivational videos and I watch at least one every day, usually in the morning. Ones with inspirational music work the best because they evoke deeper feelings. The important thing is that you do exactly what makes *you* feel motivated at least once a day. Read over your 'WHYs' every single day. If you have the type of job that allows you to personalise your work space then have motivational images and words everywhere. This will allow you to focus on motivational feelings and the images in your mind will be constantly inspirational.

FUTURE TRUTH

"I am totally committed to creating the body, finances and life of my dreams. Success is inevitable for me because I always keep going."

Now it's your turn...

TAKE A BREAK

Body Beautiful – Transform Your Body & Health

> *"Take care of your body. It's the only place you have to live."*
> **Jim Rohn**

The greatest gift we have,
Is this miraculous human body
So why is it in modern times
We are treating health like a hobby?

No matter what you love,
Good health is just implied.
Without it, fun is difficult
Ask anyone who's died

I acknowledge the fact that
This isn't possible right now
But we can show respect for those we've lost
Let me tell you how

We can appreciate our bodies,
And be healthy, fit and strong
Or we'd be disrespecting our presence here
And that would just be wrong

Enjoy yourself; of course
But the man who has most treats
Is the man who is here the longest,
By exercising and watching what he eats.

THE TWO THINGS YOUR BODY NEEDS EVERY DAY

Oxygen and water are the two things that we need regularly to operate at our absolute best. The challenge in modern society is that we are increasingly becoming a culture of dehydrated, shallow breathers.

One dramatic turnaround that I made in my life was to take conscious control of my breathing and water intake. Three times per day I engage in deep breathing that highly oxygenates my body, removes toxins and helps to relieve stress. All I do is breathe in deeply and count how many seconds I breathe in for, then I hold it for four times as long. Then I breathe out for half as long as I held it. For example, if I inhale for 4 seconds, I hold it for 16 seconds and then exhale for 8 seconds. I do this for 10 breaths and it feels amazing. It is particularly fantastic at removing that groggy feeling first thing in the morning that is caused by shallow breathing during sleep.

I also carefully monitor my water intake and I aim to eat as many water rich foods and vegetable juices as possible. This is something you can do gradually, starting straight away. You can start by committing to making sure you drink two litres or more of water per day (or whatever amount will keep you hydrated in the lifestyle you lead). You can then progress to adding some cucumber or celery to your diet. Then when you notice how great you feel, you can begin adding green juices to your lifestyle to feel even better.

I realise that the notion of green juice sounds crazy right now, and it did to me too three years ago. I can only speak from personal experience, and I have noticed dramatic improvements in my health, vitality, energy and physical appearance by drinking the juices of green fruits and vegetables like limes, cucumber, celery, and kale.

EATING TO RELEASE ENERGY

The title of this chapter is *Body Beautiful* – this is not simply meant in the sense of magazine-cover-like bodies. I mean all of your internal organs working in harmony. How beautiful is it to have your body in a position where it releases the energy required to do everything that you want to do in life!

I realised very early on that massive results needed massive energy and the way I was eating was making me tired and lethargic and activating my chronic asthma. You may be reading these words thinking "That's great, but how do I get an attractive looking body?" An attractive, *sexy* looking body takes care of itself if you are eating and exercising in a way that is optimal to your health and energy. It is then very simple to progress to enhancing specific areas of your body through targeted, muscle-building exercises.

The amount of books that are dedicated to this topic number in the thousands, and there are probably more being written and published right now. I read many of these when I was on my quest to cure myself of asthma and increase my energy levels to new heights. What I discovered was a lot of theories of optimal diet contradicted each other. The only thing that made sense to me was to try everything and see what worked best for *me personally*. I will, of course be describing the things that we all 'know' to be beneficial, like eating more green vegetables, but the most important message is to find out what foods make you feel energised and not like you need to go to sleep thirty minutes later.

EXERCISE IS FUN WHEN YOU KNOW HOW

The thing that I find amusing about exercise is that I don't have to tell you all of the benefits. You know you'll be happier, you know you'll be healthier, you know you'll look better. So why don't you do it every day?

Having just read the chapter on Massive Motivation you will have some clearer answers to this question. You are probably just attaching too many bad feelings to actually exercising and not enough bad feelings to not exercising. The chances are you are also letting your little voice take control when the time comes to exercise and you say things like "I'll start tomorrow".

I'm not suggesting you compete in a triathlon (although that would be a fantastic goal) if you are not exercising regularly right now. Starting with a fifteen-minute walk, cycle or swim would be amazing. The most important thing that you can do is to **decide** that you are going to exercise every day and then have the discipline to make it a habit. You can then build on this and there will be no shock to the system. You can build in variety and discover what type of exercise makes you feel the best. You can then build on this through the use of **goals.** You could aim to run the London Marathon in two years' time and start by taking a fifteen-minute walk around the block, tomorrow. With this goal in mind, you will gradually build up to running and then, as time progresses, increase the distance.

Unfortunately, there is no secret sauce to this. Improving your eating habits and exercising regularly is what I believe to be the only sure-fire way to become healthier, and happier with what you see in the mirror.

JUMP FOR JOY!

I'd like to tell you a little bit about the wonder of the mini – trampoline or rebounder. When I first heard about this supposedly healthy past time, I thought that it was just a fad, but as you can probably tell by now, I love researching positive results. It turned out to be one of the greatest gifts that I could have given my body and I still continue to rebound two years on. My research suggests that there are over thirty-four related health benefits to rebounding, too plentiful to describe here.

STOP AND WRITE IT DOWN

This book *is* about rapidly turning your life around so there are some highly relevant benefits listed below. To help decide that a rebounder could be for you, you can write down why this benefit would improve your life.

Benefit: Can help to decrease stress.

This will be good for me because

Benefit: Your ability to manage your BMI (body mass index) improves as well as your muscle-to-fat ratio.

This will be good for me because

Benefit: If done in the morning your energy levels could be higher for the whole day.

This will be good for me because

Benefit: Regular rebounding has been shown to decrease the breakdown of cells due to aging (you could look younger).

This will be good for me because

I have been asked in the past, how do I stay in such good shape when I eat so many avocados – aren't they full of fat? They are full of fat, but they are full of good fats. In fact, avocados are one of the most diversely beneficial foods that you can eat. My point is that it is important that you give your body sufficient good fat so that it can use it as fuel, because if you starve your body of fat, it will just store it.

Combine this with regular aerobic exercise (like running, cycling or swimming), and you are literally beginning to train your body to burn fat and operate in a more efficient way. One great by-product of this is you'll be looking and feeling great! Which is want you want, isn't it?

FEEL *PH*ENOMENAL

I have always known that I was going to write this book, even in the early days of getting out of my rut. Over time I realised that I was going to try, read and do everything so that you don't have to.

One of the things in the health and wellbeing information that kept coming up was the importance of 'alkalising'. I could write a whole book (and people have) on what this involves but it's better if I just keep it simple, isn't it?

Our blood and bodies function at their absolute best when they have a slightly alkaline pH. However, with the poor diet and high stress levels of modern society, most of us are walking around with an acidic pH. Again, I could go on to talk about scientific things for the next twelve pages but you'd prefer if I just told you how to feel better now, wouldn't you?

I have found that there are three things that we can do to alkalise our bodies so we are healthier, feel better and have much more energy. They are:

- eat a large serving of green vegetables with every meal,
- drink the juice of green fruits and vegetables (e.g. celery, cucumber, kale) every day and
- add Greens Powder (powdered vegetables) to a couple of glasses of water every day.

I can sense you are thinking that most of that sounds crazy, and I did too. It's just one of those things that you'll start doing, realise how amazing you feel after a few days, and keep doing it.

EAT LESS WITHOUT EVEN TRYING

Recently, I discovered the miracle of coconut oil. I have three teaspoons of coconut oil every day, without fail. I have personally found the health benefits amazing. One interesting benefit is that it can curb that boredom hunger where you would normally have a bar of chocolate or bag of crisps just to stop the cravings. Research suggests that this may be related to the way that the fatty acids in coconut oil are metabolised, fundamentally because it has an appetite-reducing effect.

There are also many other potential health benefits that may be caused by regular coconut oil consumption, most of which I have noticed in my life already. Things like increased energy, improved immune system, lower blood cholesterol and reduced abdominal fat, to name a few.

GET THE KNOWLEDGE THEN LIVE THE LIFESTYLE

It is crucial that you acquire the knowledge that is necessary for you to optimise your health and then act on it. Without even realising it, you could be ruining your chances of high energy and the body of your dreams. For years my Barbadian grandmother was telling me that too much dairy was no good for me as an asthmatic and someone with so many allergies, but did I stop? No. I had the knowledge but I wasn't acting on it. It wasn't until I started to acquire more knowledge and start acting on it that I really started to improve my health and body. I learned that, amongst many other things, excessive dairy consumption causes the body to produce more mucous and can be highly detrimental to people with allergies, respiratory disorders (like asthma) and regular cold sufferers. Now my dairy intake is limited to a small amount that's in certain supplements I take, or monthly 'treats'.

You will always have the free choice to eat whatever you want, whenever you want and no one can tell you otherwise. I just think that it is my duty to help you become aware of some of the things that have helped transform the health of so many people.

You may be thinking this is wonderful, but what about the beach body that I want? I can tell you right now that your beach body is inevitable if you start eating and exercising like someone who wants to live a long, full life as a starting point. Once you have done this you can then use goals that can drive you towards your ideal body dimensions. You are then back in the positive cycle of **deciding** what your body's going to look like, adopting the beliefs of someone who can get that body, acquiring the knowledge required to build that body, having a positive outlook during your training and visualising your body the way you want it, as if you have already done it. Underpin all that with **action** and your success is simply a matter of time, isn't it?

It is not easy to make the change to being healthy and looking fantastic but it is certainly simple. Either your head will be full of *excuses* that you can remove and replace with *reasons* or you can hold on to your excuses and stay right where you are. The choice is yours.

TREAT YOURSELF

One thing that is truly liberating is realising that you are having that piece of cheese, that pizza, or that glass of red wine, a couple of times per month out of choice -   rather than as a destructive daily habit. I have a client, (who we will call Cassandra for the purposes of this book) who literally swapped coffee for fruit tea, added a nutritious breakfast and stopped drinking alcohol in the week and she lost ten pounds of unwanted body fat in less than four weeks, whilst maintaining her muscle and fluids. The point is Cassandra still enjoyed a glass of wine on the weekends but she was enjoying it as a conscious treat rather than blindly chasing a good feeling out of habit, with alcohol as the vehicle.

START NOW!

In my experience the biggest obstacle people face when it comes to turning their health and body around is that they don't get started. They don't make a plan that they can stick to and take action on immediately. It's always "I can't start today because it's my dad's birthday next week", "I'll start when I've booked that holiday" or "I'll start next month". The time will never be right. You have to make it the right time, today.

STOP AND WRITE IT DOWN

If you want to, you can start turning your life and health around and improve your body right now. You can create a plan following the template below. Of course you don't have to, but if you can't stop and plan it how do you expect to actually achieve it?

I decide right now to commit to achieving the health, vitality, energy and body of my dreams.

The most powerful belief I have about getting the health and body I want is...

The daily health habits (deep breathing, water, exercise, green juices, no dairy etc.) I am excited to start are...

To acquire the knowledge that I need to be as healthy as possible, I am going to (read the following books, visit internet sites, seek out professionals, doctors, etc..)...

Draw a picture below of yourself with the body of your dreams. Have some fun with this, you can keep it private and exaggerate parts if you like.

STOP AND WRITE IT DOWN

My Primary Health and Body Goal.

It is   /   /20   ,

and I weigh   pounds / kilos

with   % body fat.

I feel amazing to be in the shape of my life and I feel energised, vibrant and extremely proud of myself.

I will achieve the this goal because (BIG REASONS)...

I am not willing to put off my health any longer.

I am committed to taking action from today onwards.

Always consult your doctor before making any changes to your diet, or starting a new exercise regime.

FUTURE TRUTH

"I have the health, body and energy of my dreams. I have a massive amount of energy that allows me to live a full successful life."

Now, write your Future Truth…

TAKE A BREAK

Time Mastery –
How to Get Enough Hours in the Day

> *"Time = life; therefore waste your time and waste your life, or master your time and master your life.*
>
> **Alan Lakein**

Time is here and then it's gone
Darkness falls after the sun has shone
As you age it goes faster and faster
And seems to be even more difficult to master
Everybody wants a piece of your pie
But you never have enough and you don't know why?
The secret seems to be, don't spend time…invest it
That sounds pretty great but here is the best bit -
Invest your time wisely and start moving towards
A life full of freedom and fantastic reward …

Jermaine Harris

It is widely accepted that time is our most precious resource. Therefore, how we use this resource (that we are so lucky to have) will have a huge impact on our happiness and success. I have spent my life having very different attitudes towards time. I started off by ignoring the issue all together, believing that I would never run out of it. I thought I could just float through life, believing that I would eventually have a great life. It is clear that I now do not believe that one can just stumble upon a great life: it, has to be created.

When I first decided to improve my life I became a workaholic, you probably know at least one person like that. There are never enough hours in a day for the workaholic; they eventually (like I did) get to a point where they realise that their health is suffering and they are not seeing their family as often as they would like, if at all.

TIME MASTERY

> *"You may delay, but time will not."*
> **Benjamin Franklin**

My aim is to be a 'Time Master'. Mastering time is the key to your overall success, happiness and fulfilment. When I say mastering time what I mean is allowing time for every aspect of your life. As a Time Master, you will be able to put in 14 hours to your business but only if that is what is absolutely required at the time.

In my quest to be a Time Master, I have found myself often getting more done in a six hour work session than in twelve. How? By making sure I not only work hard but I also work smart. You can start working smart by delegating those tasks that can be done by other people. Even if you are the only person in your business, you can hire a freelancer. You may be thinking, "I can't afford a freelancer". What if I told you can't afford **not** to hire a freelancer? Think about this for a moment. Would it not be wise to pay a freelancer £100 to complete a task for you so your time could be freed up to work on a project that could potentially generate £3,000?

FINISH TOMORROW, TODAY

During my study of the most successful people on the planet I discovered one profound but amazingly simple strategy. They were all planning everything that needed to be done tomorrow, the night before. I really started to run with this idea and I am smiling as I write these words because last night I planned to 'Write the chapter on time mastery'.

Utilising this skill allows you to visualise exactly how the next day is going to go amazingly well for you. The majesty of your subconscious mind will then begin to creatively map out solutions to any challenges that arise throughout the day. I'm sure you've also heard of the phrase 'hitting the ground running'. By planning your day the night before, you can do exactly that. By lunchtime you are way ahead of any competitors you may have because you didn't have to 'figure out' what you were going to do because it was *already done.*

DON'T FINISH YOUR 'TO-DO' LIST

In modern society we are surrounded by things that apparently demand our attention and need to be dealt with because they seem urgent. The major challenge with this approach is our time is often taken up by things that are urgent rather than things that are important. After all, when that email pops through or you get a notification from social media, you have to check it straight away, don't you?

One powerful idea that I have utilised is **not** doing everything on my to-do list. If I didn't get the chance to check my social media or watch my favourite program but I did make time to set up a potentially lucrative business meeting, write ten pages of my next book, and spend quality time with a family member, the day is a massive success.

STOP AND WRITE IT DOWN

Be very honest with yourself and write down everything that you commit time to every day. Everything from checking social media, to watching TV, to exercising, to making business calls, to serving customers. Whatever you give time to every day. Now focus on and underline the things that are most important in your life and focus on what makes the biggest difference to your success and happiness.

Decide that you are no longer willing to let the other things on your list interfere with the most important items.

JUST SAY 'NO'

I am still in the process of putting this aspect of time mastery into practice every day. It is so easy to say yes to anything and everything that comes your way because you always want to be friendly and helpful. The unfortunate reality of saying yes to everything is we have to spend valuable time getting out of things we shouldn't have got ourselves into from the start.

The best technique I have found is to say "To be totally honest and up front with you, I can't right now but if anything changes I'll let you know straight away". This allows me to focus on the things that are most important to me and stops me from adding to an already carefully balanced list of activities.

DO THE SAME AMOUNT IN HALF THE TIME

There are many situations when you could be successfully doing two things at once. You can get really creative with this and it actually becomes quite fun. I know that exercise will always be on my action plan for the day and I also know that listening to some educational material will be as well. All I do is listen to the audios whilst I'm exercising – easy. You may be committed to playing with your children every day and also want to find time to do some light exercise. Why not go play a ball game with your children in a nearby park?

Have a think about where you can make this technique work in your life and the results can be wonderfully time saving.

IT WILL TAKE LONGER THAN YOU THINK!

How many times have you allotted an hour for an activity and it has taken two? Whenever you are planning your days, weeks or months make sure to realise that things often take longer than you would like. Adopting this mind-set ultimately saves you time and any unnecessary stress. Your productivity will start to plummet as you notice the clock ticking on and on and you realise that you are going to have to play catch up with your to-do list.

When you overestimate the time it will take to do every task on your to-do list then the worst that can happen is that it will take as long as you have predicted, but most likely you will be so relaxed in the knowledge that you have enough time that you will find yourself in the wonderful position of being ahead of schedule.

LEARN FROM THE BEST AND SAVE TIME

I had no idea how to write a book, how to market a book, how to structure a book, how to speak about a book...you get the idea. This book would have probably taken three years longer to create if I hadn't sought out the people at the top of my field, purchased their books, and attended their seminars, all of which explained how to execute the whole process. Without this I would have wasted time.

It is absolutely crucial that you find a role model and find out what they did to create their success. Whatever career or endeavour you are engaged in, there is probably someone who has experienced the same journey. Find these people, interview them, buy their books, and attend their courses, because this investment of time and money in the short term will pay dividends for the rest of your life. You will save yourself, literally, years.

FUTURE TRUTH

"I am a master of time. There is always enough time for me. I always do just the right thing at just the right time. I am always in control"

Now, it's your turn...

- PART 2 -
CHANGE YOUR LIFE

> *"I want to be in a relationship where you telling me you love me is just a*
> *ceremonious validation of what you already show me."*
>
> **Steve Maraboli**

Give as much love as you can
Each and every day
So when you're gone
Your loved ones are still touched by you in every single way

Your gift of love to someone else
Is also a gift to you
Because that feeling that you give
Will return, multiplied by two

Put out the fire of anger
With feelings of adulation
An argument will finish before it starts
And you'll be back to admiration

Remember that you love them,
Really show them that you care.
After all, why would you do things on your own?
It's much more fun to share...

Jermaine Harris

Relationship Mastery – Start Caring Again

It would be great to be motivated, achieve lots of business success, and become financially free, but what if you had nobody to share it with? I have found that truly caring for, and understanding, the people closest to me to be an invaluable skill. As you become more successful you will appreciate the time and effort you put in to your relationships. Relationships are like any other aspect in life; if it is not going forwards the chances are it is going backwards. It is imperative that you become aware of the relationships in your life that you are neglecting. Think of every one of your relationships and think about what you have done over the last 30 days to add to that relationship and make it grow.

73

DON'T JUST HEAR - LISTEN

Your ears are never closed, so you will always be able to hear what is being said. However, listening and paying attention with the goal of understanding what the other person is saying is a totally different matter. Genuine listening involves maintaining eye contact, and watching the other person's body to see if they are becoming more uptight or more relaxed as they deliver their message. Listening involves repeating information back to the person to make sure you have understood the message as they intended. When you are listening properly you will not get immediately defensive if it is something that you interpret as a potential criticism.

SEE IT FROM THEIR POINT OF VIEW

Whether it is your friend, mother, father, husband, wife, colleague or employee, taking the opportunity to see it from their point of view will be the greatest gift to the relationship.

I'll give you an example. When I first decided that helping people transform their lives as a coach, speaker and author was my purpose in life, I felt compelled to leave a well-paying job. What happened next was that a lot of the people closest to me started to question what I was doing. And believe me, it really was a great job. They said I was crazy to try and make a career out of something like coaching. I had one of two choices. Either I could get very defensive and tell them they were wrong, and let an argument take place. Or, I could allow myself to see it from their point of view. When I did that, I had no bad feelings towards them whatsoever. Of course it seemed crazy. I had always wanted a well-paying graduate job, I had beaten 900+ applicants to the post, I was doing extremely well and then I left after a short time. They would be crazy *not* to think I was crazy!

Seeing the situation from their point of view meant that I could calmly sit them down and explain that this was a decision that I had made and that I was determined to make it happen. I could sit down and explain that I loved them very much and would appreciate whatever support they could give me and I would do everything in my power to live my purpose and create the best life imaginable for me and for them.

STOP AND WRITE IT DOWN

There will be a situation in your life right now where you feel like someone doesn't understand you, or it feels like they are on your back all the time. I want you to think carefully about this one, specific situation and imagine that you are the other person. Write down everything that *they* are feeling, and how *they* are seeing things. You'll quickly notice that you feel better about the position and realise that you have the power to improve the situation now that you have seen both sides.

THEY CAN'T ARGUE ON THEIR OWN

The dictionary definition of an *argument* is 'an exchange of diverging or opposite views, typically a heated or angry one'. The key word for me here is exchange. The word exchange means that two people have to be involved. If you remove yourself from the exchange of opposite views then it can't be an argument anymore. It doesn't matter whether it's your spouse or a work colleague; you can take control and turn the argument into a discussion where you can *see the situation through their eyes* and turn the argument into a discussion with an actual resolution at the end of it, rather than two angry people going nowhere.

B.P.T.R.

I know that the above approach sounds great in theory, but what action can you take to make it a reality? Whenever I feel myself on the verge of what could potentially be an argument with someone I love, or a peer, I think to myself "Come on Jermaine; B.P.T.R.". B.P.T.R. stands for Breathe, Pause, Think, and Respond.

If you had utilised this technique in the last argument you had, it probably wouldn't have even happened. Most arguments escalate to the next level because you *react* and say something that ten minutes later you wish that you hadn't. True? Do this yourself and you'll notice huge improvements with all of your interactions with other people and, most importantly, with those that you love the most.

Next time you find yourself in a situation where someone in your life says something that could create that feeling where you just want to bite back, B.P.T.R. ...

- **BREATHE** - take the oxygen in that will allow you think clearly
- **PAUSE** - allow your conscious mind to take control
- **THINK** - let the most useful, resourceful, solution-focused response come to you
- and only then should you **RESPOND**.

INTIMATE LOVE

I believe that it is important to do exactly what you did at the start of any intimate relationship, throughout the relationship. This makes it more likely that there will never be an end to it. If you randomly turned up with flowers on your fourth date, make sure you randomly turn up with an even bigger bunch of flowers three years and four months later. If you gave them a massage for no reason when you first started seeing each other, give them a massage today. Don't wait for a reason to be kind and share intimacy.

STOP AND WRITE IT DOWN

Sit back and allow all of the memories of the things that you used to do for your partner at the start to come into your consciousness. Notice some of the things that you no longer do or the things that you do once in a blue moon, and write them down so you can commit to regularly doing them again.

DAILY LOVE

It is probably becoming clear as you read this book that what you do day-to-day will ultimately impact your results. One area of life where it is easy to neglect this principle is in our intimate relationships. We forget the 'little things' that make a big difference. There are genuinely so many things that you can do every day that require little or no financial cost, that really can make your partner feel that extra bit loved. Introduce daily passion into the mix as well and long-term success is inevitable.

Personally, I like to write a little love note every single day, with a message of love, appreciation and gratitude. If you just rolled your eyes or cringed at this concept, you probably could benefit from it more than most. It is also crucial to make sure you make a big deal of the first time that you see your partner at the end of the day. Take your head out of the TV, phone or computer, and jump up and give them a big passionate kiss. This may sound like an amazingly simple idea, and I truly believe that it will make all of the difference for you.

COMPLIMENT YOUR PARTNER IN PUBLIC

We seem to have developed into a culture in which it is acceptable to make derogatory 'jokes' about our loved ones when we are around other people. How often do you hear the wife described as "the old ball and chain", "the dragon", or something similar? How regularly do you notice your friends putting their partner down in a group setting and then everyone awkwardly laughs about it? Don't get involved.

Talk about your partner with love, respect and admiration when they are around, and when they are not. This will create an amazing energy for you as a couple, and your relationship will stand out as one that is full of passion and connection.

YOU NEED GOALS

You have a goal for your body, you have a goal for your finances, you seem to have a goal for every area of your life apart from what could arguably be the most important. Think about it, we have already established that for something to make progress and improve it has to be moving towards a worthy goal.

In a relationship it is very easy to get a bit too comfortable. However, this is a dangerous state to be in, and what was once a beautiful relationship can begin to slide backwards. As with any part of our lives the easiest way to combat this is to **set goals**.

You could set a goal to take your partner on a weekend away, or to buy them flowers once a month, or take them for a meal once a week. What you do isn't really as important as actually doing something.

STOP AND WRITE IT DOWN

Make a list of things that you are going do every day / week / month / year that wouldn't cost much/any money but would take your relationship to new levels of connection and love. Even if things are great for you, what else can you do make it even better?

STOP AND WRITE IT DOWN

Set a relationship goal right now. What could you commit to achieving in your relationship that gets you excited because you know it will be great for the both of you? (If you are not in an intimate relationship, then it is also important to have goals for your other relationships so you can use the template below for a different relationship in your life).

It is   /   / 20

and I feel amazing because I have ...

.. which has improved my relationship and I feel a deeper connection and passion for...

.. than ever before.

WOMEN NEED TO VENT

Women are biologically wired to connect, and men are biologically wired to fix things. This is absolutely fine and poses no challenges as long as both parties understand how to deal with certain situations. When a woman is going through her day and certain negative things happen it is as if she has a sticky note stuck to her with a little description of what happened. By the end of the day she may be covered from head to toe in these notes plastered with things like "Sandra gave me a dirty look at work today", "I can't believe how disgusting that lunch was", and "I forgot my gym clothes so I couldn't work out".

If a wife, girlfriend, mother or sister ingested some chicken that he noticed was still raw in the middle, what would he immediately want to help her do? He'd want to help her to get it out as quickly as possible because the bacteria in the raw chicken is going to cause her pain and discomfort if it stays inside. So a male partner goes into fix-it mode automatically.

The fascinating thing is that when the women want to share all of these sticky notes they have picked up throughout the day and get them off their chest, their male partner will try to fix things straight away. Straight for the cure, that's the tactic. The real trick here is to allow her to get it all out, and all we have to do is *listen*. If she says "Will you help me do something about this?" *then* offer some thoughts on solutions, otherwise keep your suggestions to yourself!

If all of this daily emotional baggage is allowed to build up, then she'll start to hate the way she feels, and start to really feel down. It can then get to a point where there is an eruption of emotion, which is going to be explosive – and it's going to be difficult to deal with. T. The secret is to allow her to discard the negative, emotional sticky notes every single day. Then you will only be collecting a little bit at a time. If you are a woman, and you can see your man in this scenario, you may need to help him out a bit. Say something like "Honey, I've had a crazy day and I need to get some stuff off my chest. I don't need you to do anything I'd just love it if you could listen. Would that be okay?"

FINDING THE PERSON OF YOUR DREAMS

To *find* who you are looking for, you need to *know* who you are looking for. This might sound simplistic, but a lot of people don't find the person of their dreams because they simply don't know what this person is like. If you don't know exactly what it is you are looking for in a man or woman then how is your mind supposed to send you a green light when you meet someone who could be an amazing person for you to spend the rest of your life with?

STOP AND WRITE IT DOWN

You stand much more of a chance of finding a partner for life if you take the time to design what they look like, how they smile, what they do, how positive they are, what their hobbies are, and the places they like to go. Have fun right now and design your perfect partner. If you already have the person of your dreams, you can write down all of their attributes and you will also feel amazing.

FUTURE TRUTH

"*I am dedicated to constantly improving every relationship in my life. I give love, care and attention to all of my loved ones and the more love I give, the more I feel loved*"

TAKE A BREAK

The 'Rat Race' –
Do What You Love, or Love What You Do

> *"Whatever your life's work is, do it well. A person should do their job so well that the living, the dead, and the unborn could do it no better."*

Martin Luther King, Jr

I had a friend whose biggest hate,
Was the first day of the week.
Over time I realised
This wasn't really unique

Most people I speak to
Have this Monday-based affliction
The strange thing is they wanted the job
Is this not a contradiction?

I hate my job, it gets me down
Is what I often hear
"So why not starting taking steps,
To escape the pain and drear?"

"I don't know what to do?!?"
Nor does anyone when they start,
It's their passion, belief and drive,
That truly sets them apart.

By following your passion,
And making life less bleak.
You'll be truly on the road to loving every day of the week…

Jermaine Harris

If you are anything like me when I first committed to improving every area of my life, you probably have a job, and you have a passion, but they are not the same thing. Throughout University, and for a short period after, I did many different jobs that I certainly wasn't passionate about but, of course, I needed the money. The best advice I have is to continue to make the money you need from your current job, whilst getting in touch with whatever it is you can enjoy about your job, and at least work part time on your passion.

CAN I REALLY LOVE MY JOB?

If you are doing anything that does not bring you joy or happiness for a long period of time that usually indicates that it is time to make a change. When it comes to your job, this does not necessarily mean that you have to leave it. You know that right now the job is giving you the money that you need, so it is intelligent to remain in it. What you need to do is get out the rut you are in, and learn how to love your job.

PROGRESS AND CHALLENGES

How can you make progress in your job? Is there a promotion available at some point in the future? If there isn't, ask for more responsibilities so that you are learning new skills, until eventually they will have to pay you more for what you are doing, or you will have more skills to offer another employer.

It is very easy to get lost in the boring things you do every day and convince yourself that you don't want to do anything else on top of those things. However, you can easily set yourself small targets and challenges by doing more than you are paid for, and you will start to feel excited again. This is true of any job, I know because I have lived it.

For many years I was a labourer for a property maintenance company and I started to feel like a chimp could do my job. So I played a game with myself. Could I become so resourceful, so productive, and so ahead of schedule that the tradesman would notice if I wasn't there? I started making sure that everything was ready for the next phase of every job. I loved how one of my bosses would ask me for something and it would already be waiting behind him. I wasn't being paid to take this level of care with my job (nowhere near it) but it made my life so much more fulfilling, and the job that much more enjoyable.

STOP AND WRITE IT DOWN

Write down some things that you could start doing that would be a challenge for you – things that you are not paid to do. Then visualise yourself doing them and notice how you immediately feel better about yourself and your job. 74% of people actually do this exercise so well they are excited to go to work and try it out as soon as possible!

YOU ARE IMPORTANT

Whatever you do for a job, and however you have been feeling about it recently, you have to recognise that it *is* important, otherwise it wouldn't exist. Be proud of whatever you do and take the time to recognise the value that you bring to the world.

- Whose life do you make easier?
- How do you serve the greater good?
- How do you serve the public?
- Without you, what would happen?
- Without you, what wouldn't happen?

Ask these powerful questions, and you will start to get great answers.

IF YOU DON'T LIKE IT, DO IT FIRST.

Successful author and entrepreneur, Brian Tracy, has a phrase "eat the frog", which means to do the things that are going to be the most challenging, boring (or both!), right at the start of your working day. As the day progresses, your day will get gradually more 'fun' and you won't be spending your day 'dreading' those things that you don't want to do.

WHAT IF YOU WERE ABOUT TO LOSE IT?

Have you noticed that whenever someone is about to lose something, whether it's a house, a car or a job it becomes immediately more valuable to them. This is because all of the reasons why they want and need it come racing to the front of their minds.

STOP AND WRITE IT DOWN

It's time to complete the sentence "I like my job because..." as many times as you can. Your initial reaction could be "I don't like anything about my job", or "I don't like the people either". That's fine, but are you working there for free? Probably not. Do you like the fact that they pay you? Of course you do, so your first sentence will be "I like my job because... *they pay me*". Once you have the first one you will notice more start to flow - and how obvious they are. How about paid holidays? A pension? A parking space? A canteen with good food? Do you live close? Do not carry on reading until you have completed every sentence.

I like my job because

I like my job because

I like my job because

I like my job because

I like my job because

I like my job because

I like my job because

I like my job because

I like my job because

I like my job because

I like my job because

I like my job because

Now that you have completed all of the above sentences it will be amazing if you can stand up and read them just before you go to bed tonight, and again when you wake up in the morning. It is important not just to say the words, you have to feel the emotion of them. If you like your job because they pay you and that means you can provide for your family, that is wonderful. Focus on the feeling of self-worth that goes along with that. Do this every morning, and repeat it at night until you are totally refocused on seeing the good things about your job, and not obsess about the bad things, that don't really need to exist any more.

Surround Yourself with Positive People

> *"Surround yourself with only people who are going to lift you higher."*
> **Oprah Winfrey**

I should probably put this subtitle in every single chapter of the book because it makes such a huge difference to the quality of your life. It will be very difficult for you to create the new thought pattern of "I like my job" if you are surrounded by people who are constantly talking about how difficult life is, and how much they hate their job. Give yourself the gift of spending time with people who are positive about their jobs. View them as a stepping stone towards bettering themselves so they can get to the lifestyle that they truly desire.

PART TIME PASSION

Take some time to realise the things that you are passionate about in life. Make the picture in your mind of how fantastic it would be to be doing it as a full-time job. What do you see? What do you hear? What do you taste? What do you smell? How do you feel?

Really get involved with the images in your mind as you start to feel your passion increase. Whether it is helping children, speaking, writing, cooking or making clothes, ask yourself if there is someone in the world making a full-time living from doing this same thing. The answer will most probably be yes, and the people at the top of your chosen passion will be very handsomely rewarded for their efforts. I came across a woman who was making six figures per year from teaching people how to knit!

The question is never, "Is it possible?" The question is always, "Am I willing to do what it takes to make it a reality in my life?" As long as the answer to that question is "Yes" then you are in motion. Could you commit ten hours per week to starting a career for yourself in an area that you are truly passionate about? The important thing is to start with some commitment.

I started offering free coaching on the weekends so that I could hone my skills and work out what I could do to help people as quickly as possible. Then I started to educate myself for two hours per day on how to be a coach, an author and a speaker. Over time I started to do exactly what my role models had done to get to where they were, so that I could walk the same path. The very process I went through to get this book off the ground was simply the duplicating one that one of my role models had been through.

STOP AND WRITE IT DOWN

I decide now to commit to being in a position where my primary source of income comes from...

...something that I am truly passionate about doing every day. The most powerful belief I have about achieving my dream career is...

My career heroes and role models that I am going to learn from are...

The daily habits that will contribute to me gaining more skills and experience in relation to my passion are...

I am going to use the following sources - books, internet, professionals, doctors etc...

...to acquire the knowledge that I need to have my dream career.

FUTURE TRUTH

"I am so happy and grateful that I am working on my passion every day. I am proud to say that my primary source of income comes from my passion and I love every minute of it!"

THERE IS NO MAGIC PILL

If it was easy to have something you are passionate about as your job then everyone would be doing it. However, as you have been reading this book, you have become acutely aware of the value of **persistence.** If you believe that you only live once, I would love you to live it doing something that you are passionate about, whilst making money, and making a difference.

You have to be persistent with this, learn as often and as much as you can, and hold onto the picture of yourself working in your dream career on the screen of your mind every day. Find your role models, take the action, and if it doesn't work, learn from it and take new action.

BUILD A DREAM TEAM

> *"Surround yourself with people who are smarter than you."*
> **Russell Simmons**

At the time of writing, I am not exactly where I want to be just yet. I haven't spoken for 'Success Resources,' or held a seminar for over a thousand people, but here's the thing: I know I will do these things. I surround myself with people who believe I will too, and I spend time with people who are also chasing their passions. It doesn't matter what a person is doing at this present time - if they have a compelling vision of the future like you do then you can join together for the ride. Celebrate each other's successes, and pull each other back up after any temporary setbacks.

Join forums, networking websites, breakfast clubs, and attend seminars. I promise you there is a group of people who are just as passionate as you are about improving their life and operating day to day within their field of passion. Seek out these people – it's not difficult in the world we live in today, a simple internet search could be all it takes. Will it be scary to jump in and go and meet new people like this? Probably. Should you do it anyway? Of course!

I have met so many people who have been able to elevate me closer to my dreams just by attending various events and visiting community websites. Any apprehension that you feel is good, because you are breaking free into something new, and that means you are well and truly on your way to a career that you love. The steps may not be easy, but they will certainly be simple, especially if you manage your mind using what you have learned so far, and manage the money from your current job in the way you're about to learn…

Money Trouble – Money Secrets You Weren't Told – A New Money Mindset

> *"Money may not buy happiness, but I'd rather cry in a Jaguar than on a bus."*
> **Françoise Sagan**

We have already established that money will not make you happy, which is absolutely fine because that was never its' purpose. Money is just a tool that will allow you to live the life of prosperity and generosity that you deserve.

Money will only make you more of what you already are. If you are sensible, friendly and charitable, then you will become more so. If you are mean, reckless and thoughtless, then you will become more so.

One trick that really changed my life is to think of people in my life that I wouldn't exchange for £1m, and that made me feel wealthy. Do it now, picture in your mind those people that you would never dream of swapping for £1m, and notice how amazingly wealthy you feel. You are already a multi-millionaire, even if it's not in a monetary sense *yet*.

MONEY MATTERS

How often do you hear statements like "Money isn't everything", or "It's only money", or "Money doesn't mean much to me"? The fact of the matter is, money does matter. I am not saying that money is more important than anything else, I am just saying that it is sensible to recognise it as important, and an essential and inescapable component of the society we live in.

YEARS OF RESEARCH

After I had taken care of my happiness, health, relationships and motivation, I became obsessed with studying the differences between rich people and poor people. I read the books, attended the seminars and analysed the teachings. My discoveries have been plentiful, and have come from very practical, scientific teachers as well as what might be considered more 'spiritual' teachers. The thing that has fascinated me is the fact that they are all pretty much saying the same thing – to become rich, you have to think like a rich person thinks, so you can then act like a rich person acts. That might sound simple and even a little obvious, but what are you going to do about it?

I have understood the concept for some time, but I have only recently started putting things into practice, and as a result so many great things have started to happen. I always make the same joke to my friends: "I should have started with money and then improved my health and happiness". The point I am trying to make is that there are certain principles and practices that you can engage in that will allow you to make more money from various sources in a short period of time.

I have also come to realise the importance of repetition. The ultimate success of things that I am discussing in this chapter, (and probably every other idea in the book), are based on the premise that you will stay persistent and repeat the ideas to yourself over and over again with the appropriate emotion. Think of it like reprogramming your mind's software. I bet you can remember updating your smartphone recently. When was the last time you updated the software in your mind?

From a psychological standpoint, your financial situation is a result of your past programming. This is something that I really struggled with at the beginning of my journey. For many reasons I ended up being programmed to believe that it was okay to go through life with the bank balance at zero, and in using credit cards to pay for everything that I wanted. It is only through rigorous repetition that I have now started to turn this around. In my first month of formal coaching I made five times more money in a month than I had ever earned, and just a month later it was all gone.

How is it that eighty per cent of all lottery winners end up back where they were, or worse off after just five years? The answer is that something must be happening in their minds.

Become Aware of the Abundance

> *"Abundance is not something we acquire. It is something we tune into."*
> **Wayne Dyer**

It is pretty obvious that you can only benefit from things that you are consciously aware of. For example, I would not be able to benefit from the speed and luxury of an aeroplane when I wanted to go and visit my family in Barbados if the Wright brothers (and others) hadn't become consciously aware of the possibility of flight. Everything you see around you (including this book) began as a thought in someone's head, didn't it?

There is abundance all around us – the giant redwood has no limitations, it grows to its full, majestic height because that's just the way it is. If you are like me, and many other people who have turned their finances around, you probably need to address the level of conscious awareness of the potential money, wealth and abundance that are open to us all. Once you have done this you can begin to hold an image in your mind of what being financially rich would be like for you.

STOP AND WRITE IT DOWN

This next process changed my life because, once I had written down and seen it on the screen of my mind, it suddenly felt more possible. Write down, and then visualise, what life would be like if you were financially free. How you would you know? What do you see? What do you hear? What are you thinking? What do you smell? What would you taste? How amazing do you feel?

Write down everything and then visualise it in big, bright, bold pictures and hold it in your mind as long as you can.

The preceding task is one that you can do anywhere. Once you have done it a few times you will be able to make yourself feel good and believe in yourself in the blink of an eye, just by returning to this vision.

FOCUS ON MONEY

If you wanted to stop off and pick up a bunch of bananas on your way home from work, you would specifically focus on bananas and you would have a picture of bananas in your mind (like you do right now). You would go to the place in the shop where they are most likely to be stocked, and get them, wouldn't you? Why don't we do that with money? One reason is because we don't focus specifically on the *amount* of money that we truly want. How often do you hear people say "I want more money"? The truth is, I could transfer one penny into these people's bank accounts and their wish would have been granted - they'd have more money. But that's probably not what they meant. But what did they mean?

A principle that has been mentioned both deliberately and subconsciously in this book, is the idea that what you focus on expands. Over the last few years I have found this to be especially true when it comes to money. If you focus on debt and never having enough money then that is what you get more of. If you focus on the things that you already have and the abundance that is already in your life then that is what you will get more of. This is the real reason why some of the rich get richer and some of the poor get poorer and not, contrary to popular belief, because it takes money to make money. Remember those lottery winners who spent all their money?

Money will always come your way in some shape or form and you need to condition yourself to be ecstatic every time it does. Do you pick up a penny that you see on the ground? Next time, pick it up and really *feel* grateful that some unknown source is sending you money, and you will begin developing what is often referred to as a prosperity consciousness. It would be amazing if every lost penny from around the world went directly into your bank account, wouldn't it!

FUTURE TRUTH

"Amazing opportunities to make more and more money come my way every day."

MONEY MIND PICTURES

Our mind is a visual instrument - remember the bananas? Of course you do. The reason that you now see bananas in your mind's eye is the same reason as why you now see a zebra with its black and white stripes. The reason you see the things that you think about is because that's how the mind works, and you can very quickly change how you feel, as well as the success you are attracting to yourself at any given moment, by mastering this concept.

STOP AND WRITE IT DOWN

You're about to have fun realising the exact level of control you have over the pictures in your mind. Write down 10 random things (e.g. Cat, Hammer, Pen etc.) and then go back through the list and flick through a picture of each one in your mind like you were flicking through a child's picture book.

1

2

3

4

5

6

7

8

9

10

Amazing, isn't it! But what does all of this picture business have to do with money? Think about an idea that we have already discussed. Everything begins as a thought, and if a thought is an image, then everything first begins with an image.

When humans became dissatisfied with windows being covered with animal hide, cloth or wood, they built an image in their mind of being sheltered from the elements but also having the ability to see the outside world. The very moment the image was built in their minds and they decided to take action on it, what we now know as the window was inevitable. The same is true of your financial freedom. Build the image in your mind, and take action on it, and it is inevitable (as long you are persistent and prepared to adapt your strategy).

WHAT DO YOU BELIEVE?

Take a moment and think of your mind like a garden. As with any garden, there are weeds. In this particular garden of wealth the weeds are strangling any possibility of the flowers of financial freedom growing. The weeds are all the beliefs about money that you have developed over the years that do not help you become wealthy. They are things that you have heard and learned that you have internalised as beliefs. It's time to rip out those weeds right now, and regain control of your own financial destiny. Circle some of the statements below that you have heard before:

"Money is the root of all evil"
"Money doesn't grow on trees"
"Not everyone can be rich"
"You need money to make money"
"Rich people are bad"
"Rich people are selfish"
"Rich people are only interested in money"
"It's only money"

These ideas that we receive early on in our lives can subconsciously ruin any conscious attempts we make at becoming wealthy.

STOP AND WRITE IT DOWN

What do you think of, when you think about what your parents, grandparents, teachers, friends, colleagues and religious workers told you about money as a child and young adult?

STOP AND WRITE IT DOWN

Now go through everything that you may have lodged in your subconscious as a limiting belief, and write them down again, only this time write as many positive, amusing, crazy opposites as you can underneath them. For example, underneath "Rich people are bad" you could write "Rich people are amazing, charitable and keep the country going with all of their taxes".

Now you have flipped your beliefs on their head. Make a conscious, deliberate, determined effort to say the new positive beliefs to yourself at least twice per day. Do it with energy, conviction and passion, and financial freedom flowers will replace the poverty weeds in your wealth garden.

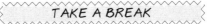

TAKE A BREAK

Money Mastery

> *"The art is not in making money, but in keeping it."*
> **Proverb**

Once you have become aware of the fact that your financial results are merely a 'printout' of what's going on inside your head, then you can really start to implement some age-old techniques that will almost guarantee you long-term wealth and enhance your short- term security.

THE FIRST PART OF YOUR MONEY IS... YOUR MONEY!

I read the concept of 'paying myself first' many times before I started to implement it, and realise its power. This was because I was still battling my old programming. I'm predicting that because you have successfully got to this part of this chapter, you have come to terms with the idea of programming at this point.

Think about this for a moment. Money arrives in your account every month, and then probably automatically starts to leave. Your mobile phone, your mortgage, your landlord, your gas, your electricity, supermarkets... the list goes on. Then you may keep some for yourself. Over the years I have realised that rich people do things slightly differently. Rich people keep 10%+ for themselves and, depending on the type of system they follow, they save it and never touch it, or they invest it in something they have knowledge of. I have started doing this and now I suggest so should you. Why? *Because that's what rich people do!*

You may have read about several different money management systems, but this basic concept is present in all of them. You may be thinking "I can't afford to take 10% out before

I even start!" The honest answer is your spending will adjust accordingly after you have paid yourself.

MY FAVOURITE SYSTEM

Next comes what I call my 'Ten Per Cent'ers' based on some of the ideas presented by one of my idols, T. Harv Eker in his book *Secrets of the Millionaire Mind* (I would also highly recommend attending his amazing course, *The Millionaire Mind Intensive*). I put 10% of every pound I earn into funding each of the following areas.

- Learning (wealthy people commit to perpetually educating themselves in their area of business)
- Future spending for things like watches, cars, holidays, etc.
- Fun & treats for things like extravagant evenings out, or massage treatments every month

I also create a feeling of balance in my life by using 5% of the money I earn to go towards my charity work. In the early months when I couldn't even spare the five per cent (although in hindsight I could have) I used to simply donate my time as opposed to the money, and in many ways the gift of time to charitable causes is a more valuable, and engaging one than just money.

The remaining 55-60% goes into my Daily Living Account that pays for everyday needs like, rent, bills, food etc.

In my Daily Living Account my debt repayment system kicks in. I was a student, and a compulsive spender for a long time, and this meant that I had debts to pay off. The absolute best way to do this was to make a plan, stick to it and send that money every month to pay off the debt and then spend the rest of my time thinking about income so I wasn't focusing on debt (what you focus on expands, remember).

MONEY, MONEY, EVERYWHERE!

What would it be like to be making money from 3, 4, 5 or 10 different sources whilst you were asleep? Think of your favourite celebrity and I can assure you that they do not make money from only one source, and the chances are they do certain things (like release a song) and then get paid handsomely for it for many years after. I know that we all may not be able to make money whilst we sleep through the same channels as Beyoncé or David Beckham. However, we can all still make money while we sleep. I believe that we should all be striving to be in a position where we are working because we choose to, not because we have to for survival reasons.

There are many techniques to help make this a reality in your life, but it would take ten books to go into them all in depth. However, there are several amazing books, courses and seminars in the 'Recommended Resources' section at the back of the book.

My research suggests that it doesn't matter what avenue you choose (Trading & Investing, Internet Marketing, Internet Business, Property Portfolios, Network Marketing, etc.). What does matter is the **decision** that you want to create multiple streams of passive income for yourself, then **learning** about how to become proficient at it and then taking **action**. There is nothing quite like the thrill of the first time you make money while you sleep.

FUTURE TRUTH

"I make huge amounts of money no matter what I am doing. I make money when I work, play and sleep. I make money 24 hours a day."

You Can Only Fail If You Stop

> *"Life is like riding a bicycle. To keep your balance you must keep moving."*
> **Albert Einstein**

When it comes to creating financial freedom, it is inevitably going to take a commitment to learning, and some persistence. However, you have the same physiology and mental faculties of all of the millionaires and billionaires out there and you can and will create the financial life you want for yourself. I am not there yet myself, and I am implementing all of the above techniques every single day. At the time of writing I am poised to make more money this month than I ever have in a whole year! I don't tell you that to impress you, just to impress upon you that when you persist in the techniques described above, and follow some simple passive income strategies, (see 'Recommended Resources' section) then you can make it happen.

- PART 3 -
CHANGE YOUR DESTINY

> "Open your eyes, look within. Are you satisfied with the life you're living?"
>
> **Bob Marley**

Build The New You –
It's Time To Live By Design

WHY ARE YOU HERE?

When I first started to turn my life around I realised that I had to become the best version of myself along the way. I had to begin to truly get in touch with who I was, why I was here, and what my priorities were. This chapter will allow you to answer those questions for yourself. This process will involve the most writing because they really are about imprinting the essence of you and your future onto your subconscious mind.

My "Why am I here?" is below, and I'm including it to show you how in-depth and dramatic you can be with this. I wanted it to be from the heart and be filled with passion, and I hope by reading mine you will write yours in a way that resonates for you, like mine does for me.

Why am I here?

I am here to humbly serve humanity by being a passionate example of the unlimited possibilities that life offers.

I am here to sincerely love everything in the universe and appreciate the miracle that is everything as well as every moment.

I am here to live life to the fullest because my life has a meaning and a purpose, and to honour this is the most powerful way to show my respect for myself and for my place in the universe. By endeavouring to become more myself I can set a strong example of what's possible for others, because I believe that you only have one life and you have to enjoy the process.

I believe that you get what you give in life, so it is important to give everything and have a passionate love affair with myself to ensure that I have more to give, because I want to reflect outwardly the gratitude I feel inside every single day. I make sure that my friends, family and loved ones are absolutely certain of my love for them.

I am here to feel excited about my life and what I can give, share and experience.

I am here to have an amazing time, create an unbelievable and inspirational story, and leave behind a legacy that grows and inspires my friends, family and future generations. I am here for those magic moments. I am here to live life on my terms. I will never settle for less than I can be, do, create or give.

I am here to be a living example of the endless possibilities of humanity. I am here to be an inspiration to others. I am here to be a role model. I am here to be remembered and leave a legacy. I am here to be a leader. I am here to create a financial situation where I have the freedom to do what I want, when I want. So I can travel the world. So I can live my perfect day. I am here to live beyond 100 years of age. I am here for health, wealth, and excitement. I am here for big smiles, to be playful, to be inspirational and to be energetic.

STOP AND WRITE IT DOWN

After reading the above, you may have noticed that your mind has started to tell you why you are here, and the reasons behind why you do what you do. Write them all down now. Include everything. Why are *you* here…?

I read the reasons why I'm here every other day, to keep them in the forefront of my mind. You will be doing something similar, as part of the final chapter, *The 30 Days that Change your Life*.

WHAT COMES FIRST?

My day-to-day life has become a lot easier since I identified my priorities, and put them in an order that made the most sense for my ultimate success and happiness. To illustrate what I mean, here are my priorities in order:

1. Health, Wellbeing and High Energy Levels
2. Family and Love
3. Laughter
4. Gratitude
5. Self-Education
6. Growth
7. Passion
8. Humility
9. Achieving
10. Investing
11. Contributing

Most people say at this point, "Surely family should be first?" I would have said the same thing, until I realised that if I didn't have my health and wellbeing then I wouldn't be in a fit state to spend time with, and look after, my family.

The wonderful thing about having an order, as opposed to a list of things that are important to you, is that there is never any conflict of interests and it doesn't take long to make a decision.

For example, let's say I have the opportunity to speak to 5,000 people that could mean a large payday and a big achievement but my Mum is taken ill all of a sudden and needs to go to the hospital. Because I know that family is above achievement in my priorities I take my Mum straight to the hospital. I know that this is an extreme example, but you'd be surprised by the conflict that people experience in these types of crunch situation. You have probably heard people say "get your priorities straight"; this is the real-life application of that phrase.

STOP AND WRITE IT DOWN

Write down your priorities in the order that means the most to you, and consider the order carefully when thinking about your ultimate success and happiness. Make sure you don't have two things next to each other that are potential contradictions. There is no right or wrong order - it has to mean the most to you.

WHO ARE YOU?

I knew that I had big dreams, and I knew that I wanted to do great things. However, who I was at the time could never make those things a reality. I had to create a vision of myself where I kept my core true, and made sure that it lived up to the best version of Jermaine Harris humanly possible. I even included things that at the time were perhaps not strictly 'true'; this gave me room to grow into this version of myself.

Once again, you may view this as a crazy thing to do, and I can assure you that all successful and fulfilled people are fully aware of who they are and who they are becoming. As with the "Why am I here?" example I have included my answer to the question "Who am I?" that I use to remind myself of every other day. Remember that I have written this as a view of my ultimate self, not from a place of over-confidence, or bragging. This is the person I am striving to become.

Who am I?

I'm an extraordinary, passionate and loving man who loves people, family, friends, animals, changing lives, and ideas that make a difference.

I love to discover and to be creative. I love nature, beaches, beautiful scenery, travel, adventure, oceans, rivers, mountains, lakes, sunshine, wildlife and breath-taking views. I am a passionate man who takes the good things in life and makes them phenomenal, and loves to share them openly, lovingly, passionately and playfully with others. I'm a massive source of inspiration. I'm a man with exceptionally high standards and excellent daily habits.

I'm a creator of possibilities, options, solutions, choices, opportunities and visions. I'm a creator of fun and laughter. I'm a creator of breakthrough moments. I'm an example of what's possible. I'm an amazing boyfriend, friend, son, grandson, nephew, mentor, strategist, personal transformation coach, internet marketer, public speaker, entrepreneur, student, teacher, author, visionary and strategic planner.
I'm fun, I'm silly and I'm playful. I'm outrageous, I'm adventurous and spontaneous.

I test the realms of possibility. I'm happy and fulfilled. I'm an athlete. I'm an author. I'm a great golfer. I'm a playful kid who can make anyone smile. I'm confident. I'm powerful. I'm masculine. I'm attractive and handsome. I'm at one with the universe. I'm a leader. I'm a great listener, I'm a master communicator. I'm committed. I'm patient.

Write your fullest answer to the question "Who am I?" Consider it from the viewpoint of who are at your core, mixed with the absolute best version of yourself that you can imagine. Notice how much fun you have with this, just like I did.

TAKE A BREAK

Your Fantastic Future – Your Exciting New Journey

> *"Change is the law of life. And those who look only to the past or present are certain to miss the future."*
>
> John F Kennedy

I often get asked, "How do I get up so early some mornings and keep going all day?" When you are enjoying the present moment and you are convinced that tomorrow is going to be even better, is there really any other way to live? The process described below is the most fun, imaginative, transformational experience I have ever gone through. It is the process that opened up new possibilities for me, and helped me to realise that many people have already done the things that I want to do, so by definition they are possible.

SILENCE THE LITTLE VOICE

Remember the exercise we did where our big voice silenced our little voice? It's time to be prepared to do that again. The minute that you start creating all of these amazing visions of the future your little voice is going to start saying things like "How the hell are *you* going to achieve something like that?" So be excited now, be bold, remove any limitations and design the future that you want for yourself, because if you don't, who will?

DESIGN YOUR DREAM DAY

Already stored in your subconscious is the script for your ideal day. As you read that you'll notice that an image of this day is starting to come to the surface.

What does your ideal day look like?
What do you do all day?
Who are you with?
How do you feel?

Write it all down right now. Remember this is your *ideal* day; money is of no object. You have no obligations to anyone else, so make sure this is written for your eyes only and not based on what someone else might think, or what you might write to please others. Please only yourself. Notice the smile on your face as the pen moves and the pictures move into your mind...

115

WORTH A THOUSAND WORDS

Everything that you desire in life has a picture associated with it. We've already talked about how the mind likes pictures and it's time to take advantage of that fact once again. It's time to find those pictures and create a scrapbook or collage so you have all of them in one place.

This can involve material things like cars and homes, dream holiday destinations, the body that you'd like to emulate, piles of cash, charity work, role models, whatever you want.

You should be excited by whatever you see, and you should be proud to know that you can achieve everything that is pictured. Do this as soon as possible.

It goes without saying that most of us want nice things in life. I have always loved cars, and I can see myself behind the wheel of a convertible Ferrari F430 in the future.

However, I have realised that as great as this is going to be, what is really exciting is the person that I am going to become (in line with my priorities) to obtain it. Once I have the keys in my hand I can be sure in the knowledge that I am a successful author, speaker, and coach who has remained loving, charitable and family-orientated while improving my finances.

Being this person is where the real excitement is, not merely having the car. Think about it, we aren't human 'havings', we are human 'beings'.

STOP AND WRITE IT DOWN

Collect the pictures of all of the material things that you would buy if you won the lottery, and realise that it is possible to get these things for yourself – if you commit yourself to it. Write down everything that comes to mind and then, next to each item, write down the type of person you'd have to become to get it.

THE RETURN OF *4-WHEEL DRIVE METHOD*™
GOAL SETTING

> **WARNING: YOU HAVE READ THIS BEFORE. IF YOU DON'T WANT TO CREATE A FANTASTIC FUTURE DON'T READ IT AGAIN. IF YOU DO, READ ON. REPETITION DEEPENS THE IMPRESSION.**

It is time to go back through the *The 4-Wheel Drive Method*™ goal setting system in almost exactly the same way as you read it before. Why? It will be strange enough to read the same thing in the same book twice, that your mind is more likely to retain the information. The only difference is that we are going to set an ultimate goal in one area of your life. This big goal will then be backed up by lots of little goals.

THE FOUR W'S

1. **W**hat do I want, exactly?
2. **W**hy exactly do I want it?
3. **W**hen exactly do I want it by?
4. **W**hat must I do to get it?

Let's start with 'What do I want, exactly?' If you don't define what it is that you want, exactly, how is your mind supposed to get you there? If you wanted to drive to your hotel in Berlin from London, would you find the exact address of the hotel or would you just type 'Germany' into the satellite navigation system? Your mind works the same way – it needs to precise know exactly where you want to go.

The most important wheel is: 'Why exactly do I want it?' You need to know why you want to achieve whatever it is that you want to achieve, and it has to be powerful enough to get you to do things that you have to do, even when you don't feel like doing them. For example, let's say that you wanted to make an extra £200 per month. If the 'Why' was "So I can pay off a bit more debt every month", you are unlikely to create much momentum and ultimately not get there. What if the 'Why' was

"So I can start my own business in an area that I have always been passionate about, and so I can eventually leave my job and do what I love every day." Do you see how this 'Why' is far more likely to create leverage and create lasting change?

Next is 'When exactly do I want it by?' You're brain needs an exact date to get you to take enough action at the right time. To use the holiday analogy again, imagine you said: "We're going on holiday next summer" and left it at that. How would you know when to pack? The answer is - you wouldn't! That is why the reality is you'd be saying something like: "We're going to New York on the 17th July 2015." Your mind would know that it has to do everything that it needs to do in preparation for the trip. Goals are the same.

The final element is: 'What must I do to get it?' This wheel has the most freedom out of all of them because you may not know everything that you have to do to achieve the goals, but it will be vital for you to take an abundance of action, and start as soon as possible! It is important that you work out what you are going to do first and find a plan, a mentor or a strategy. The most important thing is to get moving. Be careful when planning what to do to get it because if you know everything that you have to do to achieve the goal, you won't take enough action because you won't be inspired.

PUTTING IT ALL TOGETHER

Once you have gone through the above process of creating a goal you are left with something that should be phrased like the example below. Note that the goal is stated in the present tense and in such a way that evokes positive feelings of it already being achieved; this magnetises the subconscious to everything you'll need to do to achieve the goal. Once you have all of your goals written out this way it is important to review them at least once a day. I will go into detail on how to do this in the following pages.

Here is a goal that I achieved, to demonstrate how it's best phrased:

"It is February 28th 2014 and I am so happy and grateful that I easily completed my book The Rut Buster, and it is being published. This is an amazing achievement for me and it serves as a signpost in my life that I am really making happy progress every day within my dream career."

Now it's your turn.

WHICH GOAL MEANS THE MOST?

Now that the *The 4-Wheel Drive Method*^{TM} is deeply embedded in your mind, it's time for you to pick an ultimate goal in a certain area of your life, and I mean huge. Do not limit yourself at this point. Use the following areas of your life as ideas:

- Health and fitness (do you want to lose forty pounds of fat and appear on the cover of *Men's* or *Women's Health* looking healthy and chiselled?).

- Relationships (do you want to marry the man or woman of your dreams – what are they like?)

- Finances (Do you want a million, or ten million in the bank?)

- Charity (Do you want to create a multi-million pound charity?)

- Leisure (Do you want to be a scratch golfer, or better?)

These are just ideas to make you think about the type of goal we are talking about here. This is a powerful process and one that I went through in the beginning that got me to where I am today.

STOP AND WRITE IT DOWN

'What do I want, exactly?'

'When exactly do I want it by?'

'What must I do to get it?'

Now put the whole thing together as a sentence.

Notice how great it feels to have your head filled with pictures of possibilities, and dreams that are actually already a step closer to reality. You will be setting the wheels in motion towards your fantastic future in the final chapter...

The Month that Changed Your Life – Master Your Life in 30 Days

> *"Personal mastery is the discipline of continually clarifying and deepening our personal vision, of focusing our energies, of developing patience, and of seeing reality objectively."*
>
> Peter Senge

This final chapter is what the whole book has been leading up to. It is how you will approach the next 30 days so you act upon all the new knowledge you've gained. You are going to make progress towards the life of your dreams. The work you have done so far has already got you out of any mental rut you may have been in. Your eyes have been opened to new ideas and strategies that you didn't even know existed. It is now time to implement those strategies. That little voice in your head is going to have a few things to say over the next 30 days. Be prepared. Realise that it is not you any more, and make a decision to continue on the path you want to follow.

You now need to set your goals in every area of your life using the *The 4-Wheel Drive Method*™. It helps to give these goals exciting names. For example: Health for me is *'Physical Power/World Class Health, Fitness and Muscularity'* and Finances is *'Absolute Financial Freedom'*. Set goals in the following areas (you can add more) Health, Career, Relationships, Finances, Spiritual, Charity, and Contribution. Once you have set at least one goal in each area of your life you can begin the 30-day process to the life you desire. When I spoke to people about this section they said "You won't be able to get people to stick to anything as complicated as that for 30 days". I hadn't even told them what the process was! This plan is simply an outline of doing the same thing well every day for 30 days, so I only need to write it once.

I read a lot about daily routines during my personal transformation and I have spent a lot of time deciding on what I believe gets the best results, while being easy to do. It is a straightforward list of things to do based on the techniques that you have learned so far. It's so simple, fulfilling, and motivating, that the only thing that you will have to do is silence the voice in your head that tells you it's not for you. It is for you. It's for anyone.

30 DAYS TO THE REST OF YOUR LIFE

> *"Make the rest of your life, the best of your life."*
> **Eric Thomas**

Tick every box on the below list every day for 30 days (you can go to www.jermaine-harris.com/30-days to download a copy of your future truths and the checklist to print out every day).

In the Morning

☐ Get up 40 minutes earlier than usual
☐ Breathe deeply
☐ Large glass of water (with greens powder if desired)
☐ 'Future Truths' said out loud, and with passion
☐ Visualise achieving goals (feel all the feelings)

During the Day

☐ Call / text / email at least two loved ones
☐ Read something that will improve you, your life or your career
☐ Spend 20 minutes learning about a new passive income strategy

In the Evening

☐ Write a list of 10 things you are truly grateful for
☐ Answer the question "What was fantastic about today?"
☐ Answer the question "Who did I help today?"
☐ Answer the question "What did I learn today?"
☐ Plan tomorrow
☐ 'Future Truths' said out loud with passion

The most important day of this whole process is day 31. You have well and truly left your rut behind now. Are you going to continue living the old way, or instead push on to create the ultimate vision of the healthy, happy prosperous lifestyle you deserve? Of course you are... I believe in you.

CONCLUSION

I want to congratulate you on taking the first step on the journey of self-improvement. You now have the ability to decide to stay on this path and create the life that you want. It was never my intention to write a thousand-page book with every personal development idea ever written in it. I wanted to introduce you to the simplest ideas that can help you to rapidly improve your life, and I am proud to say that I think I have done that.

Now that you are on this journey, you are ready to continue your self-development. I've assembled a list of recommended books, courses and products that will allow you to continue on this journey. This is what you will find on the following pages.

Keep going and keep growing.

Free 30-Day Programme

- *7 Steps to Commit Yourself and Succeed!*
- *15 Part Audio Program, 'The Achievement Principles'*
- *7 Exclusive Commitment Training Videos*
- *The Power of Positive Thinking*
- *How to Beat Procrastination*
- *Motivational Habits*
- *How to Maintain a Positive Attitude*
- *How to Maximise Motivation*
- *10 Inspirational Quotes that can Improve Yourself*
- *10 Questions You Should Ask Yourself*
- *10 Ways to Empower Your Communication*
- *10 Ways to Start Taking Control*
- *Your 5 Minute Daily Program to Stress Management*
- *Your 7 Days Program to Positive Thinking*
- *Your 7 Days Program to Self Improvement*
- *Your 7 Days Program to Stress Management*
- *...and much, much more...*

Get your FREE programme now at:
http:// jermaine-harris.com/coaching-programme

Recommended Reading

For all of your recommended reading go to:
http://jermaine-harris.com/recommended-reading/

Recommended Tools for Success & Happiness

For your Success and Happiness tools go to:
http://jermaine-harris.com/success-tools/

The Rut Buster Seminar

For your 37% Discount to any 'Rut Buster Seminar'
http://jermaine-harris.com/seminar-discount/

Monthly Mind Upgrade

You regularly upgrade the software on your electronic devices, but
do you regularly upgrade the software of your mind?
http://jermaine-harris.com/mmu

Acknowledgements

The simple fact of the matter is that this book would never have
been written if just one of the people listed below had not been
present in my life. I truly believe that each and every one of them
has touched my life in different ways that have allowed me to
write this book.

Katie, Mum, Dad, Nan and Bampy Stevens, Nan and
Grampy Harris, Sam, Daisy, Lily and Lola: your love has given
me strength, and is still the most important thing in my life.

Andy, Lisa, Sophie and Jake, thanks for welcoming me to the
family, even though I am a bit out there. Keith and Terry, thank
you for showing me my first glimpse of how work can be fun.

Rhydian Fairfax, without your support in the early days I
would never have turned my life around. Ben Perkins kept me
accountable from all the way in Australia!

To every one of my friends who I have always affectionately
called my brothers (if you read that and smiled – you're one of
them). My Bajan family in Barbados and the USA. Your faith and
positive outlook on life inspires me. To Gran Gran for showing

me that it is possible to live for longer than a century. Mike Taylor, my Godfather. Without your support at a crucial time this book would have remained an idea.

Matt Travis, I never thought that someone younger than me would ever be such an amazing mentor, friend and business partner. I was so wrong. Avnish and Anita Goyal, Giovanni Malacrino, Melvyn John and Andrea Callanan, thank you for your deeply valued input into the book and its surrounding campaigns. David Norrington at Onion Custard Publishing Ltd.

To all of my clients, for helping me realise that this stuff works every time!

To Sarah Whitfield, the person most dedicated to constant improvement I have ever met.

Tony Bennett and the rest of the Toastmasters team. Without you, I would never have realised that I had the talent to speak about my passion.

To all of my fans and followers on social media. Your kind words inspire me every day.

To all of the greats who have mentored me over the years, some from beyond the grave. Anthony Robbins, Les Brown, Bob Proctor, Eric Thomas, Brian Tracy, Steven Covey, Michael Beckwith, Mike Douglas, Tony Gaskins, Dwayne Johnson, Will Smith, Floyd Mayweather, Joseph McClendon III, John Assaraf, Gerry Robert, T. Harv Eker, Marcus De Maria, Mac Attram, Napoleon Hill, Paul McKenna, Robert Kiyosaki, Richard Bandler, Michael Neill, Jim Rohn, Zig Ziglar, Wayne Dyer, Rhonda Byrne, Timothy Ferris, Brendon Burchard, Blair Singer, Stephanie Hale, and more…

Also to anyone and everyone else who should be mentioned here. If you have ever met me then I thank you for your input in my life, no matter how fleeting. That said, anyone who hasn't been mentioned can blame my Mum because she OK'd these acknowledgements. ☺ I thank you all.

A FINAL REQUEST

If you like this book please give it a 5* review on *Amazon,* or wherever you purchased this book from to allow me to help more people, and to qualify for my Exclusive Coaching Club.

Thank you.